ID589633

Justified by Faith

An Irish missionary experience in Malawi

For all those
who speak the truth
and are willing to
suffer the consequences

MALAWI

Songwe R.

N

Chitipa

Karonga

TANZANIA

•Rumphi

Mzuzu

Mzimba•   Nkata
          Bay

ZAMBIA

Bandawe•

L. Malawi

MOZAMBIQUE

•Mchinji   Lilongwe
            ◎

            Cape Maclear

Dedza   •Mangochi

Ntcheu•   Upper Shire R.

MOZAMBIQUE   Zomba   L.Chilwa

            Lr. Shire R. Blantyre •Magomero

            Thyolo • Ruo R.

            •Nasanje

Not to scale

Justified by Faith

An Irish missionary experience in Malawi

Angela Hanley

 St. Patrick's Missionary Society

Published in Ireland by
St. Patrick's Missionary Society
Kiltegan
Co. Wicklow

ISBN 0-9543401-0-8

Cover design by Bill Cameron
Photographs © Diana Klein *(except those the property of J. Roche)*

Printed in Ireland by Temple Printing Company Ltd., Athlone.

Acknowledgements

I am indebted to many people for their support and kindness while writing this book. To Gearoid O Brien who, as husband, has been a solid and constant support and who, as librarian in Athlone Library, made accessing research material a painless and expeditious process. To my son and daughter, Colman and Carey, whose constant interest was heartwarming. To Ita Daly who was the right woman in the right place at the right time with the right word. To Dr. Jack Mapanje who spoke freely of his prison experiences. To Kieran Birmingham, Superior General, St. Patrick's Missionary Society, whose timely phone calls were always encouraging. To Frs. Pat Byrne, Frank Taylor and Pádraig Ó Máille, St. Patrick's Missionary Society, who gave generously of their time and knowledge. To Camilla Fitzgibbon and Joan Scally who, among others already mentioned here, took time and trouble to read the draft and make helpful suggestions. Do m'anam chara, Seán Fagan S.M., whose constant affirmation and shared interest in computers has made much possible.

I am especially grateful for the generosity of Diana Klein, Catechetical Advisor to Westminster Diocese, for the use of her photographs. Bill Cameron's professionalism in the cover design was at all times inspiring. Dr. John Lloyd Lwanda of Glasgow generously granted permission to quote freely from the titles of Dudu Nsomba Publications.

Finally, I want to thank Msgr. John Roche for his co-operation and willingness to relate the whole story and for allowing me to tell the tale. Re-opening healed wounds was a profound expression of trust and I hope I have been equal to the gift.

Angela Hanley
June 2002

Author's Note

Stories of heroism are always attractive. When one considers the depths to which humankind can sink, stories of courage and selflessness remind us that the capacity for goodness is not outside our grasp. While courage in others is admirable to the onlooker, it becomes something even greater when the impetus for action is not fired by approval of others or the gain to ourselves but by the desire for truth.

When I first heard the details of Msgr. John Roche's experiences in Malawi more than a year ago while conducting an interview with him for a local newspaper, *The Westmeath Independent*, I knew that one short interview would not do it justice. This story deserved a wider audience. The story of Malawi also needed to be explored and understood and the missionary story placed within that context.

With John Roche's co-operation I conducted more than twelve hours of taped interview with him. These, together with extensive background reading, have resulted in *Justified by faith: an Irish missionary experience in Malawi*. This is not a work of history, anthropology, or politics; it does not detail the tragedy of the AIDS pandemic which deserves a complete study unto itself. This is a story, a narrative of a particular event. To understand the story of the event, however, it is necessary to understand the story of the people and how the convergence of history, politics and people in Lent 1992 set in train an extraordinary chain of events that led to the upheaval of a nation.

For those who wish to explore the story of HIV/AIDS in sub-Saharan Africa, Edward Hooper's major work, *The River: a journey back to the source of HIV/AIDS* published by Penguin, is probably the best place to start.

Introduction

"Go teach all nations...baptise them in the name of the Father, the Son and the Holy Spirit." These words of Jesus to his disciples after his resurrection inspired the beginning of Christian mission. The gospel message is a source of hope for every person. Jesus' inspiring struggle to live a fully human life, facing down evil, drawing out each person's potential and opening minds to an understanding of God's love is at the heart of missionary thinking and action.

Being a missionary is as old as being Christian. Missionary activity for the Christian believer matters because Christ matters. St. Patrick's Missionary Society has tried to express that faith conviction in its constitutions: "all people have the right to know the riches of the mystery of Christ – riches in which we believe that the whole of humanity can find everything that it is searching for concerning God, human destiny, life, death and truth. ...It is the Church's fundamental function in every age to point the awareness of the whole of humanity towards the mystery of Christ."

All this is at the core of what motivates a missionary to leave his/her own family and friends to go and live among people of diverse racial and cultural origins. Of course, there are other motivations such as the desire to travel and sample life in a culture totally different to one's own experience. In the past, there was also the condescending notion that the missionary was bringing 'civilisation' with their message of Christianity. The Second Vatican Council introduced the much-needed corrective balance to this thinking by declaring that indigenous cultures contained the 'seeds of the Word.' Inculturation has now become wholly integrated into the missionary's training and understanding of his/her mission.

Missionaries have made great personal sacrifices to reveal to people throughout the world the value and importance of Christian faith. Some have paid the ultimate price in their desire to make Christ known. The recent death of Fr. Declan O'Toole, a Mill Hill missionary in Uganda, is testimony to this. We, in St. Patrick's Missionary Society, remember Fr. Martin Boyle who was killed in Kenya eight years ago.

Missionaries are witnesses; they are messengers not the message, singers not the song. Mistakes and failures have been part of the two thousand years of missionary history. New contexts, new questions, new understandings constantly challenge the missionary. Cross-cultural living and ministry, though at times difficult and demanding, is rewarding. The majority of missionaries work among the poorest of the world's people, and are close to those who suffer. Poverty, illness, lack of education, oppression and corruption all too often mark the lives of many people today. The missionary task is to bring healing and liberation where possible. This can (and often does) bring the missionary into conflict with local political and/or other vested interests. This book narrates the dilemmas and challenges presented by the deprivations and sufferings of a people caught in a flawed and threatening political environment. I am delighted that it has been written and hope that it will strengthen the missionary interest and conviction of those who read it.

Kieran Birmingham
Superior General
St. Patrick's Missionary Society

TABLE OF CONTENTS

Prologue

Looking back towards the border at his fellow travellers standing in no-man's-land as they wept, waved handkerchiefs, and sang hymns, it was as if he had stumbled into someone else's life. He was standing where he did not belong; this could not be happening to him. This was some cosmic mistake. He was in an alternative universe where things looked real, felt real, but for some as yet unexplained reason could not possibly be real. The scene had all the ingredients of a second-rate melodrama. Like the type of film screened on Sunday afternoon, when nobody but the captive audience of the housebound is watching.

How John Roche, Apostolic Administrator of Mzuzu diocese, came to be standing in Zambia taking his final glimpse at his beloved Malawi, the land that had become his adopted country, and waving at those who, over the past twenty years, had become his family, was indeed the stuff of drama. But this drama was no soft-focus Sunday afternoon entertainment where everyone lives happily ever after. This was almost a theatre of the absurd. The sharp edge of reality that dictates that things will never be the same again had sliced through his life and left him, stunned and confused, to contemplate the result. The questions of how and why would come later. Now it was just a question of holding the pieces together, as disintegration was the unthinkable alternative.

Of course, answers to the deceptively simple questions of how and why are as complex as human behaviour itself. Did the story begin as late as January 1992 with the decision of the Malawi Episcopal Conference to write its now historic Pastoral Letter – *Living Our Faith?* Or was it in 1972 when an energetic, newly-ordained Irish missionary priest had to consult an atlas to find out where on the huge continent of Africa was a small country called Malawi? Maybe it was 1964, when Malawi achieved independence from Great Britain, ending more than 70 years of colonial rule. Any of these dates were beginnings, but perhaps 1859, the year David Livingstone steamed up the Shiré river, is as good a date as any to start for though the events are told from the perspective of one man, this is neither one man's nor one nation's story.

1

Chapter 1
A land for the taking

On New Year's Day 1859 David Livingstone, a man with a mission, travelled up the Zambezi river which he had earlier been exploring as a possible route into the African interior. From there he headed up into the waters of the Shiré river, a major tributary of the Zambezi. He had heard that this river led to a great inland sea known as 'Nyasa' or 'Nyinyesi' – meaning 'lake of the stars'. This journey was not just the result of David Livingstone's own insatiable appetite for African exploration, but was part of the wider European interest in the continent, which grew from the needs of trade and the tensions of political rivalries.

The two decades between 1850 and 1870 represented a time of accelerated growth in commercial and industrial activity in Europe. There was significant migration from rural to urban areas changing the whole profile of social life and bringing with it all the problems of sudden urban expansion in housing, sanitation and public order and organisation. The rapid expansion of the railways and the encouragement given to industry and commerce by some governments (most notably Britain and France), contributed to the sense of confidence and enterprise in those countries. This confidence and enterprise was greatly aided by capital resources of gold from both California and Australia. This together with better facilities for credit and banking and more progressive forms of business organisation, meant a rapid expansion of trade and industry in the countries of western Europe, particularly France and Britain. Germany and Italy, though mainly pre-occupied with the desirable goal of political unification, also experienced considerable economic growth.

The only two important areas of the globe not brought under European influence before 1870 were Africa and eastern Asia. This was achieved in the decades following 1870 when the rivalries and ruthlessness of European powers were particularly great. "The naked power politics of the new colonialism were the projection, onto an overseas screen, of the inter-state frictions and rivalries of Europe. It was this combination of novel economic conditions with anarchic political relations which explained the nature of the new imperialism."[1] Though Africa and Asia possessed many of the raw materials needed by industries in Europe (including cotton, silk, rubber,

[1] *Thomson, David, Europe since Napoleon (London: Penguin Books, 1978) p 494.*

vegetable oils and minerals), the need to find new outlets for the extra venture capital available and to find new markets for industrial production tended to be more important than the search for raw materials. Many of the raw materials had already been sourced by trading and without any need for political control.

Up to 1870 British manufacturers of textiles, machinery and hardware traded successfully with other European countries. After 1870, Germany, Belgium and other countries were self-sufficient in many areas and began to restrict imports by the introduction of tariff barriers. As their self-sufficiency turned into surplus, they too began to look for markets abroad. The mood of protectionism that prevailed throughout Europe encouraged governments to undertake the political conquest of what they perceived as 'underdeveloped' territories. The immense undeveloped areas of Africa and Asia looked increasingly attractive provided they could be made safe enough for investment. To this end the appropriation of these lands seemed the most obvious solution to the difficulties of the European governments.

Given the state of politics in Europe at this time, with its inherent distrust and fear between nations, and with the ever-present spectre of war, no potential advantage could be overlooked. Once the partitioning of Africa had begun, the European powers were faced with the choice of grabbing territory for themselves or seeing it taken by potential enemies. Nowhere does it appear to have been considered that the land of this great, mysterious and fertile continent belonged to its indigenous people, and was not lying there for the taking by anyone who wished to grab a piece.

Christian missionaries, too, were an integral part of colonialism. One of the most famous was David Livingstone, a Scot, who was originally sent to Africa by the London Missionary Society. He was to return later with government approval 'to open a path for commerce and Christianity' into the interior. God and mammon would be inextricably linked and loyally served by a succession of missionaries and political administrators. Their zeal is evident in the fact that in 1875 less than one-tenth of Africa had been taken from its people and made into European colonies; twenty years later only one-tenth remained unappropriated.

In 1876 Leopold II of Belgium formed the International African Association. This Association mandated the Welshman, Henry Morton Stanley, to explore the Congo on Leopold's behalf. Stanley made treaties with the native chiefs, most of whom had no idea what they were signing away, and established the influence of Leopold over vast areas of the interior. Concerned about this, Britain and Portugal set up a commission to control the navigation of the Congo river, which would restrict Leopold's access to the sea. Portugal held the colony of Angola, south of the Congo mouth since the fifteenth century and Britain now recognised Portugal's claim to control the mouth of the river. As both France and Germany had an interest in expanding their endeavours in Africa, Leopold looked to them for help in fending off the alliance of the two older colonial powers.

In order to define the 'spheres of influence' of European interests in Africa, Chancellor Otto von Bismarck of Germany and Jules Ferry of France convened a conference in 1884. Delegates from fourteen states, in effect most of Europe with the exception of Switzerland, came to the Berlin Conference. It was agreed that any power that occupied African territory and notified the other powers, could establish possession of that land. Effectively, the Treaty of Berlin (which was concluded in 1885) was an agreement among the more powerful European states to continue with the partition of Africa as amicably as possible and an attempt to separate the colonial aspirations from the political rivalries within Europe.

In the years immediately following the Berlin Conference the economic policies and nationalist pride in Britain, France, Germany and Italy favoured colonialism. Expansion into Africa was unfettered. The success of Leopold's chartered company encouraged the other colonial powers to set up chartered companies of their own. These companies were granted monopoly rights to exploit the territories that they occupied and became the means by which commerce and appropriation of African lands were achieved. Between 1888 and 1896, the German and British East Africa Companies, Cecil Rhodes' South Africa Chartered Company, the Italian Benadir Company and the Royal Niger Company were established. By these and any other means available each country established protectorates or colonies and made their resources available to the home market.

It is commonly believed that the Berlin Treaty had a decisive effect on the colonisation of Africa, that it precipitated the 'Scramble for Africa'. The reverse was actually true, the Scramble had precipitated the Berlin Conference. The race to possess Africa had started long before the conference was convened.[2] The continent was carved up among European powers without regard for tribal alliances, so lines were drawn that allied inimical tribes and divided linked tribes. The whole exercise made as little sense as it would to divide Europe as it is now constituted and recombine nationalities using the same criteria. Thus Ngoni speaking people are spread across Malawi, Tanzania, and Mozambique. The Tumbuka people across Malawi, Zambia and Tanzania and the Chewa are found in Malawi, Zambia, Zimbabwe and Mozambique.

[2] *Pakenham, Thomas, The Scramble for Africa (London: Abacus, 1994) p 254.*

* * * * *

Archaeological evidence suggests that some of the earliest inhabitants of the land that has become known as Malawi existed around 100,000 years ago. These were the ancestors of the pygmies of Central Africa and the San (commonly called Bushmen) of Southern Africa. In Malawian tradition, those who inhabited the land around the lake were known as the Kafula, a Stone Age pygmy people. They were a hunter/gatherer race and lived a peaceful existence until 2000 years ago, when mass migration of Bantu people from the area now known as Cameroon, moved through the Congo basin on to the plateaux of eastern and southern Africa. The Bantu were taller than the Kafula and well-built. They were knowledgeable in the art of ironworking and used this technology to manufacture weapons and tools. The Bantu were also skilled in working with clay and developed a distinctive pottery. Their woven baskets were of such fine quality they could be used for water storage. Dug-out canoes, perfectly adapted to the unpredictable waters of the lake, were made from msasa trees. The stability of these canoes was critical because on Lake Malawi the weather can change very quickly. Severe storms can whip up with little or no warning. Waves of more than 5m have been recorded – certainly enough to sink a small boat. One idiosyncrasy of the lake is that the waves come in threes. Both Dr. David Livingstone and his brother Charles wrote about their experiences on the lake describing the sudden storms in great detail. Charles first described the nature of triple waves: 'the seas we most dreaded rushed upon us in threes, one after the other in rapid succession. Then a few minutes of comparative calm, and another charge of three of ....these perpendicular-sided and enraged masses'[3] Lieutenant Young who came to the lake after the Livingstones said: 'The sea was past all conception: it is the peculiar nature of this lake to raise a sea that could only be found ... in the Atlantic.... It is impossible to describe the awful combinations of whirlwinds, thunderclouds and lightning that seemed to throw the lake into the wildest fury.'[4]

Like the Kafula, the Bantu people were also hunters but as they had developed the skills of cultivation, they could grow their plant requirements. As a result, they lived together in communities of villages and were more settled than the Kafula. It would appear that in the main, the Bantu people lived peacefully with their neighbours, and eventually became the dominant group in the area. Some local stories would suggest that relationships were

---

[3] Ransford, Oliver, Livingstone's Lake: the drama of Nyasa (London: John Murray, 1966) p 253.

[4] Ibid. p 254.

6

not without their problems: "the Katanga [Bantu] hated the Kafula because the latter were so small, acted like thieves and cut the legs of their captured enemies."[5]

Early Portuguese explorers, who reached the area in the early sixteenth century, recorded a powerful kingdom called Maravi which covered much of southern Malawi as we know it today, as well as parts of what are now Mozambique and Zambia. The Chewa and Nyanja people would seem to be descended from the Maravi

Between the fourteenth and eighteenth centuries, yet more Bantu migrations occurred and northern Malawi was eventually settled by the Tumbuka, Phoka, Lambya and Ngonde people. During the nineteenth century, two more significant migrations occurred. The Yao people from western Mozambique invaded the southern highlands of Malawi. As they moved through, they killed the more peaceful inhabitants of the country or sold them into slavery. The Yao were armed by Arab slave traders and were responsible for the capture and sale into slavery of many Malawian people. The Ngoni were a displaced Zulu people who, among many others, were scattered by a very powerful Zulu king, Shaka, of what is now South Africa. While the Yao happily sold their prisoners into slavery, the Ngoni, on the other hand, though also a powerful, warlike group, tended to integrate the conquered tribes into their own communities as they moved through the territory.

While slavery and trade in slavery had existed in Africa for many centuries, it was only in the nineteenth century that demand from the Middle East considerably increased the need to supply slaves from eastern and southern Africa. Slaves captured in western Africa were used to supply the American and Caribbean market.

The conditions endured by the unfortunate captives were appalling. They had to endure a forced march to one of the Arab slave-trading centres. They were usually chained or tied to wooden poles that were fashioned to fit around their necks. Many were also forced to carry elephant tusks, as ivory was a valuable trading commodity. Any potential slaves who became ill and unable to make the journey were simply abandoned to die by dehydration or to be killed by wild animals. The death rate on these forced marches was high. In the estimated forty million black African people 'exported' to the New World, those who died in tribal warfare during slave raids, on the marches, awaiting transportation in the ports or on the ships, are not taken into account.

[5] Rafael, B.R., A short history of Malawi (Limbe: Popular Publications, 1988) p 14.

When the captives reached the trading centres, they were sold to a wholesaler. They were then loaded onto sailing boats, Arab dhows, and brought across Lake Malawi for the onward march to the ports of the east coast. When they reached the coast, they were again packed on dhows for transportation to Zanzibar. This was a large Arab city-state trading centre which became an important import/export centre for the movement of goods between the African interior and the states around the Indian Ocean. The centre also included a slave market as the slaves were very much a saleable commodity.

Having endured all the terrors since their capture, the slaves had now to undertake the appalling conditions of the journey by sea to the Arab ports. The people were packed tightly, lying down, into the hold of the boat. They were held in place by the tiers of people above them. They were lucky to have three feet clearance between the tiers. In some cases, it might be less than eighteen inches. For the duration of the journey, they would have neither food nor water. They also had to lie in their own excrement. If journeys took longer than anticipated because of weather conditions, any of the people who died could not be removed until the boat reached its destination. Though they did not realise it, help for the slaves was on the way. Unfortunately, that help was to create a whole new set of problems that would have long-lasting implications for Malawi.

On New Year's Day 1859, David Livingstone steamed up the Zambezi happier than he had been in months. The Zambezi exploration had proved to be a disaster. Not having explored the lower part of the waterway properly in an earlier expedition, Livingstone set off in 1858 with great confidence and significant government funding to open a trading route to central Africa via the Zambezi. Very soon he realised that it was not just a matter of finding the most suitable channel through the swamps of the delta, which alone took three weeks to discover. For the next four months they struggled along the waterway, suffering the effects of heatstroke and fever, as they hauled their boat over endless sandbanks, unloading and reloading their stores every time. Eventually, the expedition reached the Kebrabrasa cataracts and realised they could go no further. The waters of the Zambezi, 'God's Highway' to the interior, had defeated them. Contemplating the disaster that faced them and the embarrassment that waited at home in England for him, Livingstone decided to abandon the Zambezi expedition and explore one of its tributaries, believing that God had put these obstacles in his way to cause him to take a new direction. He decided on the Shiré, which he had heard led to a magnificent inland sea: 'the lake of the stars'.

Livingstone was totally captivated by his first sight of the valleys and forested hills and with the variety of wildlife that roamed among them.

Credited as he is with the 'discovery' of Nyasaland, a German explorer almost beat him to it. As Livingstone was approaching from the south, Albrecht Roscher was heading towards the land from the east. Roscher was young, only twenty-two, and inexperienced. His expedition was poorly funded and as a result he wasted a lot of time trying to engage porters for the journey inland. In the end, having met with little success, he decided to join an Arab caravan setting out to hunt for slaves. During the journey he was poorly treated by the Arabs; he was quite ill with fever most of the time. He eventually arrived at the shores of Lake Nyasa a mere 72 days behind Livingstone.

As he was busy exploring the Shiré Highlands, it would not be until 16th September 1859 that Livingstone would set eyes on the immense fabled lake of the stars. He did not actually reach the shore of the lake itself until 17th September. His discovery of the lake was second only in importance to his discovery of the Mosi oa tunya waterfall in 1855, which he renamed Victoria Falls after the British monarch. Coinciding with Livingstone's arrival in Nyasaland as he called it, were the first of the Arab funded slaving parties. As Livingstone and his group only had time to spend one night at the lake, they spread their blankets between the branches of a huge banyan tree. Nearby, a large slave caravan had set up camp. The Arab traders came to talk to the Europeans and among the items they offered for trade were three little black girls at little more than a shilling each. In his letters to his friends Livingstone tells them that the slave trade is an affront to God, and stamping it out must be a priority.

David Livingstone never reached the farthest end of the lake, nor even saw it. At the time he was surveying it, there were war parties of Ngoni in the region and Livingstone's companions, including his brother Charles, were in a state of near mutiny from fear. He decided that the mountains he could see ahead closing in on the lake represented its furthest extremity. He did not realise that the northern tip of the lake curved a little to the west beyond the mountains that jutted into the lake. To the end of his life, Livingstone believed the lake to be 100 miles shorter than it actually was.

In 1861 Livingstone was delighted to hear that a group of Anglican missionaries with a bishop to lead them, had left England and were on their way to Africa aboard the vessel Pioneer. Livingstone and the bishop, Charles Frederick Mackenzie, met for the first time in early February 1861 and the two became close friends. After the bishop had settled in, David Livingstone, in the company of his brother and another sailor set off to explore the lake. The bishop had set up his mission at Magomero in the area of high ground north-east of the Shiré river. He had a ready made congregation when a group of slavers, startled by the sight of the white men, abandoned their captives and ran off. This group was enlarged by another band of liberated slaves following an armed confrontation between Yao slave traders and Livingstone's party. A pacifist by nature, Bishop Mackenzie, seeing the actions of the slavers around them, eventually took up arms against them. The missionaries burned Yao villages and killed those who resisted them. He organised an expedition to follow an unrepentant chief. This delayed his rendezvous with Livingstone, who was on his way back from the lake. They were both to meet the boat that was carrying Mackenzie's sister whom he had persuaded to join them. Unfortunately, he arrived at the meeting point too late. He and his fellow missionary, Mr. Burrup, camped on an island waiting for the steamer's return. It was not long before the two men were overcome by fever and after three weeks' illness, the bishop died on 31st January, 1862. His companion managed to struggle back to the mission at Magomero, where he died three weeks later. Following Mackenzie's death, other missionaries came and built new missions in the Lower Shiré area, but they endured terrible suffering from malaria and other illnesses. Eventually they had to leave and they went to Zanzibar, off the east cost of Africa.

Lieutenant Young who had travelled with David Livingstone, and was later part of the first Livingstone Search Expedition, was asked to lead a return of the missionaries to Central Africa. He returned to Lake Nyasa in 1875 with Dr. Robert Laws from the Free Church of Scotland. They built their new Mission at Cape Maclear, a headland on the southern shore of the lake, which was subsequently named Livingstonia after the explorer. The missionaries believed that they had picked a good healthy, quiet and well-protected place. They developed the mission and built schools, but had very little success in making converts. A second group of missionaries came in 1876 to reinforce the efforts of the first group in the north. By 1881 several of the young missionaries had died from fevers; the area, being malarial, was not as healthy as originally thought. In 1881 the missionaries, struggling to survive, decided to abandon the settlement and move to Bandawe much further north on the western shore of the lake. Unfortunately for the beleaguered missionaries, Bandawe also proved most unsuitable, so in 1894, the Livingstonia Mission uprooted for the third and final time and moved to higher ground between the eastern escarpment of the Nyika plateau and the lake. After initial tensions with the Ngoni, not the least of which were concerns about the cause of death of the paramount Chief M'mbelwa's son. When he was visiting Chief M'mbelwa, Dr. Laws laid his hand on the boy's head, complimenting him. When the boy died some time later from some unspecified illness, the witch doctor said that Dr. Laws had put his hand on the child's head and said: "So high, and never higher," meaning the child would not grow any more. Fortunately, with Dr. Laws' inherent respect for the local people, and Chief M'mbelwa's good sense, they overcame their differences and the missionaries eventually settled and carried on with their work. The Livingstonia Mission, under Dr. Laws, became the foremost college providing a European education to the Africans of Nyasaland. It educated large numbers of teachers, hospital assistants, preachers and eventually civil servants. Dr. Laws also provided a vocational training along with the more academic education. The education of women was also a priority for Laws, a fact not always appreciated by his contemporaries, or his successors.

Around the same time a third group of Scottish missionaries, from the Established Church of Scotland settled in the south of the country in the area of the Shiré river. They were led by Henry Henderson who had helped Young and Laws settle at Cape Maclear when they attempted to start the mission there. Despite their religious differences, the two church groups co-operated well. This mission in the Shiré Highlands was called Blantyre after the birthplace of David Livingstone. Blantyre continued to grow and thrive and became the bustling commercial capital it is today. As in the north, this mission had its difficulties in the beginning, chiefly because of the almost total ignorance of the missionaries of long-established cultural practices of the indigenous people. While some of the earliest missionaries made some attempt to understand the local people, as time went on and more and more missionaries arrived, there was less interest in learning the customs of the original inhabitants.

The Presbyterian missionaries were not the only ones to experience difficulties. In 1889 the Catholic religious order, Missionaries of Africa, arrived in Malawi. They had been founded in Algeria in 1869 by Cardinal Lavigerie. They became known colloquially as the White Fathers because of the Arab-style of their dress. By 1875 they had spread to Tunisia, and by 1878 were active in the Belgian Congo. The Missionaries of Africa arrived on the shores of Lake Malawi in the Mangochi district. As did their Presbyterian brethren, they too suffered from illness and difficult living conditions and faced the hostility of the local Yao chief, Mponda. Quite demoralised, the missionaries eventually left, after only eighteen months, to settle in Zambia where they founded the Mambwe mission.

Some time later, Bishop Dupont of the Missionaries of Africa was home in France on sick leave and persuaded a friend of his younger days, Pierre Bourget of the Montfort Fathers, to attempt to re-establish a mission in

Malawi. In July, 1901, the Montfort Fathers arrived at Nzama near Ntcheu. This was the first permanent Catholic mission in Malawi. The White Fathers returned to Malawi in September 1902.

∗ ∗ ∗ ∗ ∗

In narratives of the exploration and settlement of Nyasaland, the Yao are shown to be a fierce and warlike people. The Ngoni, while appearing less aggressive than the Yao, are also mentioned as being a warlike tribe by the white explorers. Yet to consider just one aspect of the culture of the Ngoni, their child-rearing practices, it becomes obvious they were not in any need of the white man's 'civilisation.'

All Ngoni children, male and female, remained in the village world of the women until they were about seven years old. As soon as they were able to walk, the children left the house to enter the broader world of the village. This was still the women's world, but larger than what they had been used to. There was an understanding that the children were the responsibility of the whole community, to be praised or chastised as needed by anyone in the village. If a child passed by a group of adults, courtesy insisted that he or she walked in front of them body bent forward, saying 'I am before your eyes'. The lesson of this training was *ulemu*, which meant honour/respect/politeness. The concern for training was taken seriously. Rudeness, unkindness, lack of generosity, bragging, pestering, failure to speak up respectfully were dealt with by a suitable proverb (being the gentlest chastisement), an open rebuke or physical punishment, depending on the seriousness of the misdemeanour.

The Ngoni believed that character was partly inborn and partly formed by training. They watched for the inborn qualities of children – the *mabadidwe (nature)*. They knew that along with positive qualities, some children had innate antisocial qualities: cruelty, meanness, jealousy. They hoped to correct these by *makhalidwe (nurture)*, training in human relationships.

Many of the children ran about naked until about the age of four or five. They were kept meticulously clean as the Ngoni set great store by cleanliness. By the age of four or five, the children were fully toilet trained and were able to go into the bush and relieve themselves. Although the naked children played together, they were watched carefully for signs of sexual exploration and this was discouraged. When they were about five years old, the children were clothed and trained in modesty. Around this time they started sleeping in huts with the other children, away from their parents. When they were about seven years old, the boys went to live in all-male dormitories until they were married. Here they mixed with the older boys and started their training in men's work. The girls remained in the women's area forming their own groups.

When the missionaries arrived, the Ngoni justifiably resented the suggestion that they were an ignorant or uncivilised people. Their traditional culture included a reckoning of time and the seasons, astronomy, a number system, an oral history and an oral code of law. Despite their antagonism, the Ngoni began to see that the centre of the invader's power was their system of education. They eventually conceded to letting their children be educated in the European way. In the mid-twentieth century, during anthropological fieldwork, an Ngoni administrative officer told the anthropologist, Margaret Read, that he took his son out of European school at the age of eleven and sent him to live in a village dormitory. The father explained: "There are two kinds of education: book learning in school, and learning how to live with people. I learned this last in my own boyhood when I was herding cattle, and I do not want my son to miss out on that education. He can come back to me later and go to high school, and then choose what he wants to do."[6]

Though enthusiastic missionaries from many denominations flocked to Africa, as time went on, the Christian message became a very mixed message indeed with the lack of respect and understanding of social structures of the people. Early missionaries denounced polygamy, dress codes and many tribal practices, including some ritual dancing. Authentic morality for the African existed in the relationship of the individual with his family, based on respect rather than fear. Through the family connections the individual was connected to the tribe, to the ancestors and also to the unborn. Land for them was not something to be owned and guarded jealously. What the land had to offer in terms of harvest could be owned, but land itself was part of everyone, for everyone.

In their evangelising, the missionaries brought not only a foreign faith system, but a foreign culture to which the new faith system seemed to be inextricably linked. The segregation that existed socially and politically was also religious, with the scandal of separate worship for black people and white people. Inculturation was totally unknown in the nineteenth and the first half of the twentieth century. As Sr. Anne Nasimiyu-Wasike stated in her paper delivered at a theological symposium held in Rome to complement the Synod of Bishops for Africa in the Spring of 1994: "The Northern Church for a long time looked upon the rest of the world as needing salvation and

[6] *Sheldon White and Barbara Notkin White, Childhood: pathways of discovery (London: Harper & Row 1980) pp 23-25.*

civilisation. .. Evangelisation of the world was carried out through the northern models, which included cultural forms, patterns and processes. ..Humanity in the northern culture has tended to identify many specifically Northern cultural traits as basic human characteristics. For example, Greek-Roman logic was considered proper logic and the abstract style of the classical Greek thinking as the highest developed human thinking. Those who did not think the same way were branded as 'pre-logical', 'primitive' or 'pre-scientific'. Therefore, the emphasis was placed on the need to civilise these peoples in order to evangelise them."[7]

---

[7] Anne Nasimiyu-Wasike, L.S.O.S.F., "Africa and the north: dialogue of solidarity," In W. Von Holzen and S. Fagan, eds., Africa, the kairos of a Synod (Rome: Sedos, 1994) p 135.

— Chapter 2 —
Colonisation

In the 1880s as the appropriation of African land by European powers went on apace, Britain, at the behest of its missionaries, and as the dominant power in the area of Lake Nyasa, was anxious to keep at bay the claims of Germany and Portugal, both of whom had interests in the region. With the withdrawal of British naval ships from the coast of East Africa, the slave trade had also increased. All these pressing concerns encouraged the British Foreign Office to believe that their interests needed protection in the area around Lake Nyasa. The Foreign Office was happy to allow Cecil Rhodes' British South Africa Company to invest in and administer the area of the Shiré Highlands at the southern end of the lake. Rhode's company employed the services of Sir Harry Johnston, who was already in position as commissioner and consul-general for the lands under British rule at his administrative base in Zomba, in the Nyasa District.

The Portuguese were less than happy with Britain's claim to the land around the lake and sent an armed expedition of about 3,000 men to the area. Johnston met the expedition with the threat of war between Portugal and Britain. The leader of the Portuguese went back to Quelimane, Mozambique, for further instructions, while his second-in-command attacked the Kalolo people north of the Ruo river. Following this, the British declared the area of the Shiré Highlands and the country up to the lake to be under their protection. The western territories adjoining Lake Nyasa were then added to this and the Nyasland District became a British Protectorate. The eastern coastline of the lake became part of the Protectorate in 1914.

In 1891 Sir Harry Johnston, who had formerly been the British Consul in Mozambique, was appointed the first commissioner of the Protectorate. Johnston made a concerted effort to stamp out the Arab slave trade, and to this end, as well as ensuring the safety of British trading interests, he made treaties with a number of chiefs along the lake to the northern end. The skirmishing between the Portuguese and British was finally ended with an Anglo-Portuguese Treaty signed on 11th June, 1891. This agreement fixed the north-western boundary of Malawi at the Songwe river. The north-eastern boundary had already been fixed in a previous agreement, the Anglo-German Treaty, signed on 1st July, 1890. In 1893 the Nyasaland District Protectorate became the British Central African Protectorate.

Between 1891 and 1895 Johnston applied himself to stamping out the slave trade. This brought him into conflict with strong Yao chiefs in the south who worked with the Arabs. After a number of battles and defeats, Johnston eventually overcame the Yao and they agreed to stop co-operating with the Arab slave trade. In Johnston's eyes there remained only one obstacle to the elimination of the slave trade and that was the powerful chief Mlozi in the north. In 1895, Johnston felt ready to challenge him in his own territory and after a tough battle Mlozi was wounded, eventually defeated and captured. He was tried by a number of Ngonde chiefs under the chairmanship of Johnston, sentenced and hanged. During 1896, following his victory over Mlozi, Johnston, in a show of strength, sent armed expeditions to a number of chiefs to ensure that they would submit to British rule. Even after Johnston had left the Protectorate, chiefs of the Ngoni were forced to submit to the Crown in 1898 and 1904. In 1907, the British Central African Protectorate became Nyasaland with all responsibility for its administration transferred to the British Colonial Office.

The way was now open for even greater settlement of Europeans in Malawi. Ruled as it had been by a commissioner who approved all decisions himself, there was no structured civil/government service. As there were not enough professionals available, former traders, soldiers, big game hunters and missionaries were taken into the service. Law and order was the province of Government, while health, education and agriculture were the bailiwick of the missionaries. The country was divided up into four districts at first, and then into twelve. The district commissioner represented the government in the district and was responsible for collecting taxes and custom duties. He was also head of the police, in charge of the court, and the district post-master.

As European settlement increased, the demand for land also increased. Huge tracts of land were bought at very low rates from individual chiefs. People whose families had worked the land suddenly found themselves considered tenants of the new landowner. People who were freed from the risk of slave capture, suddenly found themselves considered a source of labour for those who took over their land. With the European settlement came the introduction of money. Prior to this all trading among the local people was carried out by barter. Money was then introduced to pay the taxes demanded by the government. A poll tax of six shillings per year for each male was introduced. This was a crippling tax on a population that had no resources to provide it. When tax-collectors, accompanied by soldiers, called to the villages to collect the tax, those who could not pay saw their huts burned down. Eventually, after several representations to

Johnston by the chiefs and missionaries, the individual poll tax was changed to a hut tax and reduced to three shillings a year. For very many people this was still way beyond their ability to pay. Three shillings was the amount paid to an estate labourer for one month's work. Those who could not pay their tax could work for one month on an estate to earn the money.

In 1901 when the estate-owners were short of labourers, they agitated for an increase in the hut tax. Alfred Sharpe, who was commissioner at this time, (he became Governor in 1907 when the protectorate became Nyasaland) raised the tax from three shillings to twelve shillings per hut. If the men worked for one month on a planter's estate, they were told that they would only have to pay half that amount. Though the African people were already used to paying a tribute to their chief, the European way of extracting tax was different than the African way. While the chief had a right to the tributes, he also had the responsibility of the protection and well-being of his people. The Europeans did not operate the same reciprocation.

Before the planters arrived, land was owned by the whole community and individuals looked after their own family needs. They paid their tribute from their produce. With the settlement of African land by Europeans, as tenants the local people ended up owing rent. Those who could not pay (a significant number) were required to work for the rent. This was known as *thangata* and was little more than forced labour.

The burden of the hut tax forced many Malawians to look for work in other countries. Thus started a haemorrhage of migrant labour that was to continue right through the colonial period and beyond. Prior to the European take-over of their land, most Malawians lived their lives almost totally in their own villages. It is estimated that by the 1950s, Malawian men were leaving their homeland at the rate of 150,000 a year to work in the mines and on the plantations of Rhodesia and South Africa. Apart from the obvious disruption of family life, in a strongly patriarchal society where functions and duties were very clearly delineated, women head-of-households would not have been accorded the same respect as their male counterparts. By the 1980s and 1990s, the migration was to have a very significant impact on the health of the population of the country as a whole when the HIV/AIDS pandemic took hold.

When brought under the auspices of the British Colonial Office in 1907, the office of commissioner became that of governor. Under the governor two councils were created: a legislative council which made the laws and an executive council which enacted them. The Chairman of the legislative council was the governor. The six members consisted of three government officials and three representatives from the missionaries, the planters and the traders – one from each category. The single missionary representative was expected to look after the interests of all of the Africans, who had no representation in their own right. The governor was also the chairman of the executive council, whose three appointed members were all government officials who were also the members of the legislative council. Because the African system of governance was not understood by the Europeans, African leaders were not included in the system of administration, nor were they even considered for administrative posts, even though there were not enough experienced European officials available to serve.

In 1912 a limited form of African administration was introduced. Each district was divided into units (usually of seven). Each unit comprised a number of villages. A principal headman was appointed to oversee each unit. He was assisted by two councillors who were chosen from the village headmen. This was not the introduction of democracy for the African though, as the principal headman could not make rules and had no responsibility for collecting taxes, which was done by the district officials. They could arrest lawbreakers, but if cases were to be tried according to tribal law, they could not take place without the consent of the district ruler. In appointing principal headmen, many of the traditional chiefs were overlooked, therefore these government appointees commanded very little respect from the people, neither were they trusted enough by the British to be taken into government administration. Having no say in the government of their own country, or even their own districts, it was hardly surprising that the seeds of rebellion had been sown among the people of Malawi.

The name John Chilembwe will immediately spring to mind when considering the martyrology of Malawi. He is credited with leading the first rebellion against the foreign colonial power in his country in 1915. However, we must go back to 1892 to find the influences that were to be brought to bear on him and direct him to his first and fatal clash with the authorities. In 1892, the Rev. Joseph Booth, a British Baptist minister, set up his independent mission in the Shiré Highlands near Blantyre. Booth had the aspect and vigour of an Old Testament prophet and began preaching in the area along the lakeshore in 1893. He was sympathetic to the plight of the African and many flocked to his sermons. He was also a contentious and opinionated man, and it was inevitable that he should come into conflict with the neighbouring missionaries and the ruling authorities who eventually deported him in 1902.

In 1908 Elliott Kamwana, a Malawian from the Tonga people, returned to the country having worked in the South African goldmines. In South Africa he had come under the influence of Rev. Joseph Booth whose fiery oratory and evangelical zeal greatly inspired him. At the time Kamwana met him, Booth had, himself, come under the influence of an American draper, Pastor Charles Taze Russell. Russell had put his business acumen to work for him so that his evangelical pursuits were generally profitable, whereas Booth was always in financial straits. When he met Booth, Russell's latest venture, The Watchtower Bible and Tract Society, was proving particularly profitable.

Kamwana was a fervent disciple of the Watch Tower movement and his bible-thumping style of preaching drew huge crowds to his open-air services and hundreds presented themselves for baptism. He continually exhorted his congregations to return to the African tribal customs and a rejection of the teachings of the established missionaries. He often ended his sermons by railing against the taxes imposed by the government. He implied that refusing to pay the taxes would have very little retaliation as he believed the Second Coming of Christ would occur in October 1914. In the new order that would then exist, there would be no place for Europeans in Nyasaland. Needless to say, the government took a very dim view of what they regarded as his seditious rhetoric and expelled him from the country. Rev. Booth had meanwhile aligned himself with another religious grouping, so with his defection and Kamwana's expulsion, the Watch Tower movement declined in Nyasaland. The decline was aided and abetted by Russell, the founder, who had become entangled in divorce proceedings because of alleged misconduct in Pittsburg with women of his congregation. Further trouble was to ensue when he was implicated in a scandal where he was promoting, profitably it must be said, a 'miracle wheat' seed. *L208537*

Though Booth and Kamwama had both been deported, nevertheless, while they were in the country their oratory had struck a chord with the ordinary people, not the least of whom was John Chilembwe.

John Chilembwe's origins have been speculated on by a number of people. His own account says that his father was a Yao from Mangoche Hill at the southern end of the lake, who captured his mother, a Mangaja, in a slave raid. She escaped from Chilembwe senior and gave birth to her son, John, in 1871 at Sangano, a village near Mount Chiradzulu. As a youth, Chilembwe wrote a note to Joseph Booth asking for employment. He was immediately engaged as a kitchen boy. Given his intelligence and ability, it was not long before John Chilembwe became Booth's friend. Chilembwe was baptised by Booth on 17th July, 1893. For four years they travelled the country together establishing mission stations. Eventually, capricious and volatile as ever, Booth fell out with his supporters and decided to go to America with Chilembwe to look for funding for his African mission. Longfoirt

The American experience was seminal for Chilembwe. In Virginia, he found himself in African-American circles that were critical of the white men and the history of their treatment of black people. Feeling more connected to the American blacks than to his white missionary mentor, Chilembwe parted company with the Rev. Joseph Booth and, financed by a black church, he entered a seminary. Three years later he graduated and returned to the land of the lake a fully-fledged and politicised clergyman, with enough funds to pay £25.18s.0d. to purchase outright ninety-three acres of land adjoining the estate of Alexander Livingstone Bruce, the Doctor's grandson.

As the political situation became more stabilised from the white settlers' perspective, in 1893 Mr. Bruce, a Scottish businessman who had married Agnes Livingstone, bought a large tract of land at Magomero. Their son, Alexander, settled the land and within four years over three hundred square miles were reclaimed from their natural state. William Jervis Livingstone, another member of the Doctor's extended family, was appointed manager of the estate. Other planters took land around the Bruce estate and none of the white settlers were happy with John Chilembwe's purchase. Confident of his own ability, Chilembwe developed his mission at Mbombwe despite the attitude of the Europeans, who snubbed and avoided him. By 1912, he had a significant number of converts and 1,000 children attending his mission school. He had built four permanent outstation churches as well as a number of grass huts where services were held. At the mission itself, he built a huge brick church.

Chilembwe, a versatile and adaptable man, worked extremely hard. He preached and he taught. He planned building projects, he attended meetings. He was involved in everything that concerned his people, from organising boycotts, to attending women's sewing classes. He was a man of his people. More importantly, he was able to demonstrate that an African could match any endeavour of the European.

For as long as Chilembwe confined himself to missionary activity, he was just about tolerated by the European population. However, when he started to offer advice to the planters on how they might improve their relations with the black labour force, they perceived him more as a fomenter of trouble. As he continued to be fully confident in his own ability and unintimidated by them, their suspicion of him hardened into unmitigated animosity. Of all the white planters in the area, William Jervis Livingstone, the manager of the Bruce estate, was the most unpleasant to Chilembwe. Livingstone was a successful estate manager, not least because he disciplined his work force severely and got as much work out of them as possible for the least recompense. He disapproved of their wearing European-style clothes and resented the fact that they attended church services on Saturdays, which meant he could not work them on that day. He was quite indignant that the workers should erect grass churches on the estate, and it was not unusual for him to burn them down. The commission that was later to inquire into the Rising, and by no means sympathetic to the African, found that Livingstone's practices with regard to the African workers on his estate were 'unduly harsh' and 'in several respects illegal and oppressive.' It was hardly surprising, therefore, that Chilembwe's rebellion should become focused on his white neighbours and particularly on William Jervis Livingstone.

Chilembwe not only had suggestions for the planters in their labour relations, he was also critical of certain government policies. He was particularly angry at the forced conscription of African men into the British colonial army at the outbreak of war in 1914. The breaking-point for him was the spilling of African blood in a European war at the battle of Karonga. (German East Africa (later Tanganyika) bordered Nyasaland on the north and north-east frontiers) He wrote to the Nyasaland Times giving vent to his anger: *'In time of peace, everything for the Europeans only. And instead of honour we suffer humiliation and names contemptible. But in time of war it has been found that we are needed to share hardships and shed blood in equality....the poor Africans who have nothing to own in this present world, who in death leave only a long line of widows and orphans in utter want and dire distress are invited to die for a cause which is not theirs'*[1] Even though it only had a tiny circulation, the issue of the *Nyasaland Times* in which this letter appeared was suppressed by the government.

Given Chilembwe's confidence in his own African identity and the treatment of his fellow countrymen by the European colonists, it is hardly surprising that his attention should turn to rebellion. He gathered around him a band of eager followers and began to plan. Even though his rebellion was local, he had enlisted a provisional promise of assistance from the German occupants of Tanganyika, (to become Tanzania in 1964) on the age-old premise that 'my enemy's enemy is my friend.' The plan he eventually worked out was quite straightforward. On the night of 23rd January, 1915, three groups of armed men were to set out from Mbombwe. One was to go directly to Magomero and kill the white men living there. Another group was to go to another residential area of the Bruce estate and deal with the white occupants in the same way. The third group was to march on Blantyre, raid the arsenal there and return with the guns and ammunition to

[1] *Ransford, Livingstone's Lake: the drama of Nyasa, p 229*

Mbombwe for the next stage of the plan. Chilembwe was confident of support from some of the Ngoni in Gomani. A number of headmen in Zomba also told him that their people would support the rebellion. Strict orders went out from Chilembwe that no white women or children were to be harmed. The order was obeyed to the letter.

On the fateful night, a group of silent spearmen approached the Livingstone household. William Livingstone was attacked and overpowered. He was decapitated and his head impaled on a stake. His assistant, McCormick, was also killed. The third white man was not to be found as he had gone to Blantyre for the evening. Livingstone's head was borne aloft as the men returned to Mbombwe with the women and children from the estate as hostages. The second attack on the other residential area of Mwanje resulted in one of the two white men being killed. The other was wounded but managed to escape with his wife. The third prong of the offensive, the attack on the arsenal, was completely bungled. The discipline seems to have been less effective than in the first two attacks. After a fifteen mile hike across country to Blantyre, the rebels only managed to grab a few rifles and rounds of ammunition before they were disturbed by sounds from the Gymkhana Club nearby. Thinking the sounds of revelry meant an impending attack, the ill-disciplined group panicked and scattered. Four men were captured and were executed in public the following day to discourage any other hopeful rebels.

The group that had captured the hostages at Magomero arrived back to Mbombwe on Sunday morning. It is said that Chilembwe conducted his church service with William Livingstone's head on the altar. By Monday, it became clear that the uprising was a military failure. The supporting rebellion of the Ngoni and the village leaders in Zomba was put down with relative ease. Despite this, reports of the uprising spread amongst the European population like wildfire, with grossly exaggerated tales of wholesale slaughter. By Monday evening, government troops were closing in on Chilembwe. His supporters, deciding that discretion was the better part of valour, slipped away towards the Portuguese border. Chilembwe seems to have been quite sanguine about this desertion by his men. He ordered that the hostages taken at Magomero be taken from his village and left where the pursuing troops would find them, shocked but unharmed. One of the last acts of the fleeing insurgents was to seriously injure a priest and burn down a Catholic church the Nguludi Mission which happened to be on their way to the border. The impressive brick church at Mbombwe was dynamited by government forces, thereby removing a potent symbol of local African achievement. Chilembwe eluded immediate capture but while hiding out in a village he was betrayed by one of his own countrymen for the bounty on his head. He was shot dead on 3rd February, 1915, without benefit of court or trial.

Even though the colonial powers had finally got rid of the one man that was most likely to be a serious threat to their ambitions, the fact that the revolt should have happened at all raised serious problems for the Blantyre Presbyterian Mission. Over eighty of the rebels had been baptised members of the Mission. This raised suspicions in the colonial administration and among the white planters that the educational policy of the Mission was directly subversive. A commission of inquiry was set up. In the legislative council, Alexander Livingstone Bruce, the owner of the Magomero estate, proposed that all schools where 'native' teachers were in charge should be closed.

Unable to view the rebellion as a serious indicator of deep flaws in the colonial system, the ruling powers considered it proof of the need to reinforce the colonial position and keep the 'native' population firmly in its place. Alexander Heatherwick, leader of the Blantyre Mission, was called before the Commission of Inquiry on 29th June, 1915. The following extract is cited in an article, "Crisis and Identity: Presbyterian Ecclesiology in Southern Malawi 1891-1993," by Kenneth R. Ross[2]:

Commission: Can any native get a Bible?
Heatherwick: Yes, we will sell it to any native.
Comm: Do you think the native, educated or otherwise, is capable of understanding the Holy Scripture?
H'wick: Yes, as capable as any ordinary Christian.
Comm: Do you think the Bible in Chinyanja [also Chewa - one of the local languages] is clear and understood?
H'wick: Undoubtedly.
Comm: If a teacher selects an isolated portion or verse, may he not misapply it?
H'wick: Yes, as a European might.
Comm: We have it on evidence that native teachers do sometimes discuss amongst themselves texts from the Bible.
H'wick: And why not?
Comm: Can the native interpret it correctly to others?
H'wick: The native is as able to interpret the Bible as you are.

[2] *Missionalia: Journal of the Southern African Missiological Society.* *23:3 November 1997. pp 381-397*

Heatherwick's admirable defence of the local people is seen further when he was questioned about responsibility being given to local black people.

Comm: You say there may be 12 Europeans and 10 natives [on the ruling body of the church]. Soon the native vote may have the majority. Are you prepared for the Church of Scotland practically to be governed by a native majority?

H'wick: It may be.

Comm: Is there not a danger of giving the native so soon such power?

H'wick: We have seen nothing of the danger as yet and I fear none.

Comm: Do you think the result of mission education is to lose a sense of respect for Europeans? Have you found this?

H'wick: I have had respect from every native I met.

Comm: Of course natives get swollen heads!

H'wick: As Europeans do – we have met them!

The questioning concluded with a complaint that the Africans showed disrespect to the Europeans because they did not doff their hats when they passed them. Heatherwick responded in character: *'I have seen many Europeans absolutely ignore a boy's* [sic] *salutation. The smallest drummer boy in the British army if he salutes Lord Kitchener receives a salute in return. There will be no difficulty if the European makes acknowledgement: it indicates that two gentlemen have met and not only one.'*

While there was a significant connection between the Blantyre Mission community of believers and John Chilembwe's uprising, not all the African leaders approved of it. One such was Harry Kambwiri Matecheta. He had been ordained to ministry within the Mission in 1911. While distancing himself from the rising, he had no difficulty in expressing his difficulties with the colonial rule in an essay to the Commission of Inquiry. He wrote: *'We know that at Magomero* [the Bruce estate] *they were persecuted for attending Church, or for building a small grass hut for prayers. Why? We do not know, and that the case came to the hearing of the Resident at Chiradzulu, and instead of putting the matter right, one of the natives was put in prison three months with hard labour.'*[3]

The Chilembwe Uprising, like the Easter Rising in Ireland in 1916 was a military failure, but like the Easter Rising, it was an important symbolic success and laid down the foundational layer of the matrix that would give rise to a powerful nationalist consciousness over the following decades.

[3] *ibid.*

— *Chapter 3* —

Political awareness

With education given by the missionaries, the African people learned the ways of the European and began to look for ways to make their voices heard. They had become teachers, civil servants, clerks, farmers and ministers of religion. In some cases, these people were appointed by chiefs to act as advisors, but given the differences of values and priorities between the system of tribal education and the European school system, acting as advisors did not always work well. Eventually, a group of the European-educated Africans decided to organise themselves into groups called 'Native Associations.' The main aims of these associations were to create the means whereby there could be two-way communication between the African people and the colonial government, and to organise public meetings where matters of particular interest to the African could be discussed.

A small number of Europeans, particularly Dr. Laws of the Livingstonia Mission was supportive of these Native Associations. However, it was he, and not they, who laid down the guidelines for the organisation of the Associations.

These were:
1. The members of the Associations were to be of good character.
2. They were to be educated (in the European manner) and loyal to the Government.
3. The Government should approve their membership.
4. The Associations were to hold their meetings in public
5. Their minutes should be sent to the top Government officials.

Only one organisation could deal directly with the Government; this was the Representative Committee of the Northern Native Associations which was formed in 1924. It represented quite a number of civil servants who worked in Zomba near the heart of Government. The district commissioner or his representative was present at the ordinary meetings of the Associations. The minutes of their meetings had to pass through Native Authorities and District Councils. If this didn't happen, no action would be taken on any recommendations. This limited discussions at the meetings, which included concern about war-widows who were in dire poverty;

migrant labour; improvement of roads; marketing opportunities; price control; increase of financial support of education; and the provision of secondary schools by the Government. It was inevitable that members of the Associations resented the lack of freedom to associate. At one meeting it was agreed that all the land in that part of the country belonged to the Africans and no more should be taken and settled by white people. The government began to look suspiciously at the Native Associations.

Two very influential and active men in the Native Associations were James Sangala and Levi Zililo Mumba. Mumba was a particularly talented and able man. He was the first African member of the Advisory Committee for Education, appointed to the position in 1933. The committee was established in 1926 as a result of an investigation by a visiting commission from London into the state of education in Nyasaland. Mumba appreciated the need for secondary education for the African population which, at that time, was only being offered in the Livingstonia Mission in the north of the country. His repeated requests for such education was ignored for many years until the arrival of another visiting commission, after which money was made available for more secondary schools. It was 1940 before a secondary school opened in the Blantyre Mission. This was followed in 1942 by Zomba Catholic secondary school operated by the Montfort Fathers.

Levi Mumba visited South Africa with a Government mission. While there he saw that the Africans had organised themselves in the South African National Congress. When he returned he worked, in the northern region, towards a strong political union of the Africans in Nyasaland. In the south James Sangala was working to the same end. Together with Mr. Bandawe, they founded the Nyasaland Educated African Council in 1942, concerned mainly with the improvement of education for the African. Out of this grew the Nyasaland African Congress, established in 1944, which was more political and was concerned with all matters that affected the African. Levi Mumba became its first chairman. This was the first national organisation to look after the rights of the indigenous people of Nyasaland.

In the years following World War I colonial occupation throughout Africa continued to increase. In Malawi, the numbers of white settlers was low in comparison to other countries, chiefly because there were few natural resources to be exploited. By independence, there were a total of 8,000 white Europeans in the country, most of whom arrived in the 1940s and 1950s. Racism had now become a factor in European colonisation. While the attitude of the original settlers and missionaries might have been patronising and ignorant, regarding the African as we might a child, it was not usually racist. After both World Wars, the number of white settlers in many of the colonies increased. People who would have had very little at home, suddenly found themselves with large tracts of land, big houses, servants and no idea how to behave towards the indigenous African. Racism did not only exist among the nouveau riche but it was also alive and well amongst the professional classes. Dr. Austin Mkandwire in his book *Living My Destiny*, describes encounters with British doctors sent to replace those who had resigned in protest at the federation: "*most of these new recruits had been brainwashed into treating Africans as inferior. They had quickly learned to loathe Africans and they willingly demonstrated their antipathy against Africans on the flimsiest excuse.*" Even with those who would readily work with the African, there still was not total acceptance of the black person. Mkandawire tells of another experience with an Irish doctor who "*was loved, revered and almost worshipped by the Africans, to whom he was dedicated and with whom he formed a special relationship.*" This doctor also showed tremendous respect to those Africans with whom he worked. Yet on one occasion in 1951, when Mkandawire, a favoured student of the doctor, was helping the doctor scrub up for an emergency procedure, he accidentally put the doctor's boots on the wrong feet. "*He merely looked at me and said 'Austin, what do you think you have done?' I looked down but could not detect the mistake I had made. And so he stood there and repeated the question. ... He was furious and he kicked me in my ribs as I bent down to detect the mistake.*" Both men met in Ireland in 1966 where Mkandawire was training in an Irish hospital. The doctor apologised for his brutish behaviour, saying that he was deeply sorry and that it should never have happened.

Also while not openly declared, as in South Africa, there was a de facto apartheid system in operation. Lilongwe was divided up into areas according to race – the whites living in the more developed and prosperous areas north of the river, all others in the south. Since the administrative centre was in the northern part of the city, the colour bar did not apply during the day, but after dark Africans and Asians could not cross the bridge from south to north without proof of being in transit. There were separate African and European hospitals in Zomba. Any Europeans in the African hospital had European doctors from the European hospital to attend them.

After Germany's defeat in World War I, the Allied powers, through the League of Nations divided up its colonies and the Arab provinces of the Ottoman Empire between them. However, at much the same time, there was also a rise in political movements opposed to colonialism, particularly in Egypt and India. In sub-Saharan Africa, things were moving a lot more slowly. In Northern Rhodesia and Southern Rhodesia, there was no movement at all.

In the early years of colonisation, the white farmers in Southern Rhodesia, anxious to consolidate their position, looked first towards South Africa, but after the defeat of the Boer by the English, they looked closer to home to Northern Rhodesia in which rich mineral deposits, particularly copper, had been discovered. If the countries united, the development of agriculture, mining and industry would yield immense wealth for the white settlers. The white settlers of Nyasaland were also very interested in the idea of federation with both the Rhodesias, though the governor, Geoffrey Colby was opposed to the idea, believing that Nyasaland would gain least while losing even greater numbers of its active men to migrant labour within the federation. This would have considerable effect on the white-owned estates. The concerns of the black population were not even considered.

A number of commissions were dispatched to investigate the possibilities of federation. In 1938 the Bledisloe Commission reported that they encountered strong opposition towards any amalgamation or federation among the indigenous Africans. White racism was a very strong feature of Southern Rhodesia where many of the people of Nyasaland went to work, and as bad as the attitude to the black people was, they felt it would be worse in federation. There was also the concern that new white settlers would arrive to take away yet more of their land. The Africans were also very aware that the struggle for independence which was stirring all over the continent would be set back by federation.

Over the years of World War II, the plans for federation were shelved. When hostilities ceased, the white settlers under the leadership of Godfrey Huggins in Southern Rhodesia and Roy Welensky in Northern Rhodesia, ensured that negotiations re-commenced. A number of conferences were held at which there was no African representation. The Colonial Secretary, James Griffiths of the Labour Party, in London realised that African support was important. He had his officials prepare a draft Constitution for the federation. One of the aims was that the interests of the Africans in all three countries be safeguarded. To do this, it was suggested that there be a Minister for African Interests, and an African Affairs Board. The minister would be the Chairman of the Board. This board had to examine all federal laws before publication to see that they did not damage African interests. According to the Colonial Office, officials in all three countries were supposed to explain to the people what federation would mean. That the administrations in all three countries favoured federation meant the supposed impartial campaigning left much to be desired.

James Griffiths visited Central Africa himself and met with a delegation from Nyasaland National Congress Party under its leader Mr. James Sangala, and with Chief Mwase. Chief Mwase told Griffiths that his people did not want federation, as it would only benefit Europeans, who would want more land, more wealth and more power. Griffiths assured the delegates that Malawi would remain a Protectorate and would not be amalgamated, which was a very real fear, with the other countries. The delegation was invited to further discussions with white Europeans at Victoria Falls. Sangala declined, probably realising that he was wasting his time. While appearing to have made a sincere effort to dialogue with the affected Africans, at no stage does Griffiths appear to have listened to them, or considered dropping the proposal of federation in face of such strong African opposition. The decision to federate seems to have been implicit all along; the only outstanding matter was how to do it in the best way possible.

In Britain, the General Election of 1951 ousted the Labour Party and brought the Conservatives into power. Oliver Lyttleton was made Colonial Secretary. He had less regard for the African than Griffith, supported the racist attitudes of the white Europeans, and was convinced of the benefits of federation to the white settlers. Matters proceeded quite quickly from there on; a constitution was developed and a bill was prepared for Parliament. A number of chiefs, still believing that they had some say in the matter, hurried to London to prevent the passing of the bill. The Colonial Office would not give them a hearing and they were prevented from presenting a petition to the Queen. The bill was passed in Parliament, despite strong opposition from the Labour and Liberal parties. The Federation of Rhodesia and Nyasaland received the approval of the Queen on 1st August 1953 and became a reality.

At a meeting in Blantyre in 1953 the Chief's Council and the Nyasaland African Congress joined forces and founded the Supreme Council of Chiefs and Congress. They decided to oppose the Federation by passive resistance. The first expression of non-co-operation came from Chief Mwase, when he refused to attend the coronation of Queen Elizabeth II. Another chief, Gomani, advised his people to ignore government directives on forestry and agriculture. Gomani was ordered by the government to withdraw his suggestion, but he refused. The chief was arrested and expelled. The passive resistance then erupted into violence and there were riots in Thyolo, Blantyre, Zomba, Mulanje and Nsanje. The government called in police reinforcements from the two Rhodesias as well as Tanganyika, (which was now in British hands following the defeat of Germany in the war). Eleven people were killed and seventy-two wounded. A further two people were killed at Domasi when local people had gathered to support their headman when he was arrested. As a result of the resistance and unrest, the government dismissed many black civil servants and deposed tribal chiefs. Seeing the effects of the government clamp-down on their people, the organisers decided to end the passive resistance. The Nyasaland African Congress was having its own internal difficulties, which weakened it as a cohesive opposition to the Federation.

1953 saw another event take place that was to have an impact on Malawi far greater and for far longer than Federation. An African medical doctor who had lived and worked in London, moved to Ghana. The doctor, Hastings Kamuzu Banda, was a friend of Kwame Nkruhmah who had also returned to Ghana from London. Banda had known Nkrumah and other African intellectuals who were to become part of the independence movements in their own countries, when they all lived in London in the 1940s. Banda was seen by those working for independence within Nyasaland as the obvious choice to unite their efforts. He was an older man in a society that revered the wisdom of age. He was an educated man. He was a man who had experience of studying, living and working abroad. Many of the other leaders in Africa were also coming home from abroad, educated in the manner and ways of the white man. And, most importantly Dr. Banda was deeply opposed to the Federation. His cause was vigorously championed by the young men within the Nyasaland African Congress, whereas some of the older people were concerned that he had been away too long and was out of touch with the African way of doing things. The energy, enthusiasm and charisma of the younger men won and Dr. Banda was invited to return to Nyasaland.

A number of key government departments of Nyasaland came under the responsibility of the federal government: income tax, audit, health, civil aviation, post and telegraphs, prisons, non-African and higher education, and defence. Any remaining departments were administered by the Nyasaland government. When the health portfolio was seconded to the Federation it had a significant impact on the training of medical auxiliaries. The Christian missions, particularly at Livingstonia and Blantyre made education a priority. As early as 1881, the Bandawe mission had discovered the usefulness of having paramedics with some medical training. The formal training of paramedical staff began in 1894 at Livingstonia under Dr. Laws.

The first hospital assistants' training course with government recognition was set up in 1909.The hospital assistants' course was spread over three years. In year one, the subjects studied were: chemistry, osteology, pharmacy, biology, anatomy and physiology. In year two: anatomy, materia medica [the remedial substances used in the practice of medicine] and therapeutics, surgery, clinical surgery, pathology and bacteriology, public health, toxicology and medical jurisprudence – theoretical and practical and clinical medicine. In year three: systematic medicine, midwifery and clinical surgery. In 1926 a registration scheme for hospital assistants was set up by the Medical Council. As the value of the trained paramedic became more obvious, the three-year course was extended to four years, so that the hospital assistants could act as doctor substitutes when necessary. The fourth year was spent doing practical work in medical, surgical and laboratory procedures, nursing, theatre and anaesthesia. The students sat for the Nyasaland Hospital Assistant Diploma which entitled them to practise medicine, surgery and midwifery.

When the Federation assumed responsibility for health matters in 1954, it strictly limited the curricula of the Hospital Assistants' Course, and reduced it to three years. The resulting qualification did not entitle the holders to practise medicine as they had heretofore.

While the Federation was pushed through in the face of bitter opposition of the African people of the three countries concerned, it already contained within it the seeds of its own destruction. The new Conservative Government concluded discussions on Federation and designed its constitution in haste. Government responsibility for the Federation was divided between the Colonial Office, responsible for Northern Rhodesia and Nyasaland, and the Commonwealth Relations Office, responsible for Southern Rhodesia and the Federation administration. With this separation of responsibilities, it was almost impossible to develop a coherent and effective policy of federal government. By the time a Secretary of State for Central Africa was appointed in 1962, the inexorable roll towards de-colonisation and independence had begun, and it was too late to achieve anything other than the orderly dismantling of the Federation.

Three men held the post of Governor of Nyasaland during the time of federation: Geoffrey Colby, from 1948 to 1956, Robert Armitage from 1956 to 1961 and Glyn Jones from 1961 to 1964.

Colby was opposed to the creation of the Federation and worked vigorously to prevent it. He had worked on the development of the economy of Nyasaland and believed that it could function independently of the resources of the Rhodesias. He also believed that there was a serious lack of goodwill towards Nyasaland in Southern Rhodesia. Realising that Federation was inevitable, he secured the best possible financial deal from the British Government for Nyasaland. He also successfully resisted any attempt to expand the federal responsibilities to include crop marketing, public works and the creation of a federal police force. Early in his administration Colby appointed the first Africans to the legislative council –

Ellerton Mposa and Ernest Muwamba. Some years later the first Africans were elected to the council – Henry Chimpembere, Kanyama Chiume, N.D. Kwenje, Ralph Chinyama and Dunstan Chijozi.

When Armitage succeeded Colby in 1956, his chief task, as instructed by the British Government, was to win over the indigenous African people to the Federation. He knew that this would only happen if the discriminatory laws and practices existing in the country were outlawed. It was also necessary that Nyasaland be guaranteed a fair share of the federal development budget. A believer in the promotion of Africans in the civil service, in 1959 Armitage appointed the first African members of the executive council: Mtawali and Chinkondenji. A new constitution was agreed in 1960 which introduced elections. With the election, a majority of Africans was voted into the legislature; this meant that four Africans and a European sympathetic to the African cause could take their place with ministerial status on the executive council. There was now an equal number of elected African and appointed European members on the council. In 1963 under the last governor, Sir Glyn Jones, full internal self-government was brought about as the nominated members were all eventually replaced by elected members. H.K. Banda became Prime Minister, overseeing a cabinet of nine ministers, seven of whom were African with one pro-African European, Colin Cameron, and one Colonial nominee, Henry Phillips. Phillips was eventually replaced by John Tembo when Independence was granted.

Chapter 4

H.K. Banda

There are various dates given for the birth of Hastings Kamuzu Banda. It is likely to be anywhere between 1902 and 1906. He was a bright child and learned to read and write while employed as a domestic servant by the missionary Dr. Prentice. He showed such promise that at the tender age of thirteen he went to the Livingstonia Mission to train as a teacher. When he was sitting a teacher's examination he was expelled for cheating. Banda was a small slight youth and it is said that in order to read the questions, he stood up from behind a large burly student in front of him to look over his shoulder at the blackboard. The supervisor of the examination interpreted this action as an intention to cheat and expelled him from the examination.

Deeply shamed, Banda had to leave the Mission. Hoping to continue his education, he left home in 1915 and walked to Hartley in Southern Rhodesia. There he worked as a hospital orderly and continued his studies in the evening. In 1917 Banda and his uncle Hancock Msokera Phiri left Rhodesia for South Africa. He worked in the mines, first in Mafeking and then in Johannesburg. He continued, as before, with his studies in the evenings. He was very fortunate to get the opportunity of a scholarship from the African Methodist Church, which had been intended for his uncle. Phiri, deciding he was too old, gave his nephew the chance of a lifetime. In 1925 he travelled to America to begin his second-level studies at the African Methodist Church's Wilberforce Institute in Ohio. In 1930 he entered the University of Chicago and in 1932 enrolled in the Meharry Medical College, Tennessee, to study medicine. He graduated in 1937. Knowing that he would not be able to practise medicine anywhere in the British Empire without a British medical qualification, Banda enrolled in the School of Medicine in the Royal College of Physicians and Surgeons in Edinburgh in 1938.

When he received his British medical licenciates, he hoped to go back to Malawi to practise medicine. However, his efforts were frustrated by the reluctance of the white doctors and nurses to work with him as an equal. (Africans could work in the hospitals as hospital orderlies or hospital assistants). Having spent some time in Liverpool, he was sent to work in Tyneside during World War II because he declared he was a conscientious objector. In Tyneside his job was to look after the foreign seamen. After the war, Banda made his way to London and settled into a comfortable life there. In the course of his life in London he came in contact with many politically active Africans who were working towards independence of their countries. In 1953, Banda moved to Ghana. He seems to have left London under a cloud, with some suggestion that he was about to be struck off the medical register. In Ghana he lived with a woman, Mrs. French, with whom he had a son. He also got himself in trouble with the medical authorities in Ghana and was suspended for a period of five months.

Around this time, the Nyasaland African Congress was finding its voice and had attracted young, western-educated and eager men. Banda supported them ideologically and had given some financial assistance from London. He was also generous in his hospitality afforded to any of his compatriots who visited London while he lived there. He was building up a reputation as an opponent of federation, and his willingness to speak out on this while living in the very heart of the colonial power impressed those in the Nyasaland African Congress. His education was also a very significant factor in the admiration of his fellow countrymen who appreciated the value of such education.

The younger men within the Nyasaland African Congress were anxious to change the leadership of the party, which they regarded as being too conservative. They were looking for somebody who would have broad appeal and unite the various strands of the party. Ethnically, culturally, linguistically, there was a broad spectrum of peoples contained within the colonial borders of Nyasaland. For example, there were (in no particular order and not exhaustive) Ngoni, Tonga, Tumbuka, Lambya, Lomwe, Ngonde, Yao, Nyanja/Chewa. They needed to fight colonialism with a united voice. To them Banda seemed the obvious choice – he was a well-educated, travelled man, familiar with the white society of Europeans and Americans. Kanyama Chiume, public secretary of the Nyasaland African Congress was an exceptional publicist. He knew that he would have to 'sell' the idea of Banda to the population at large. He set about this task with great energy and skill. As he and others toured the country they built the character of Banda into messianic proportions. He was presented as the country's saviour. All sorts of stories that fitted in with the oral tradition were created about him – that he was invincible, that he was immortal – bullets could not hurt him, poisons had no effect on him. A whole myth was created around him. Chiume was spectacularly successful with his campaign and when Banda returned to Nyasaland on 6th July 1958, he received a hero's welcome. His hands were repeatedly kissed and he was swathed in animal skins over his western-style suit.

Banda found all this attention very much to his liking and settled into the role of 'saviour' very quickly. His highly emotional style of oratory appealed to the masses, and his anti-federation litany seemed to be what they needed to hear. He seldom failed to leave his audience shouting their approval of him. Oddly, he always spoke in English and was to do so right throughout his presidency. He seemed tireless in his travels up and down the country consolidating his support base. In August 1958 he was accepted as leader, on his own terms, of the Nyasaland African Congress at their conference held at Nkhata Bay. The constitution of Congress was amended to give Banda sole power to appoint officers of the party and the members of the executive council. Given the manifest intelligence of the young cadre in the Nyasaland African Congress, it is a little puzzling as to why they allowed Banda to set the parameters of his power without any checks. Perhaps they saw him as an old man, unlikely to stay in power for very long, and his presence would prevent any leadership struggle among the 'young guns' until the country established its independence. As it was, by allowing him to assume total control, they presented Dr. Banda the noose with which to hang them.

In the months that followed, he vowed to smash the Federation. The United Federal Party was the dominant European party in the Federation and refused to co-operate with the Government and would not bring forward any proposals for constitutional change, unless its own narrow self-serving desires were granted. It wanted the federalising of non-African agriculture. These delaying tactics angered the Nyasaland African Congress and contributed to the unrest that was ultimately to lead to the state of emergency in 1959.

After a brief visit to Accra, in newly independent Ghana, around Christmas 1958, where he was taken to task for the lack of any proof of serious rebellion in Nyasaland, Banda returned in a much more aggressive mood. His followers picked up on the mood, and secret meetings were held to discuss the overthrow of government. Banda's rhetoric encouraged the African population and there were disturbances in many places throughout the country. As the violence worsened, a decision was taken to arrest Congress members. On 3rd March, 1959 a state of emergency was declared and in 'Operation Sunrise' hundreds of Congress members were arrested. Banda himself was also arrested, without any struggle, and detained in Gwelo prison in Southern Rhodesia. The government forces met with surprisingly little resistance throughout the country, except in one area in the north.

Nkhata Bay was known to be a stronghold of the Nyasaland African Congress. On the morning of 3rd March, the district commissioner in the town, in accordance with the instructions given to him, arrested nine members of the Congress and held them in the local gaol until the steamboat M.V. Mpasa arrived at 6.30am to collect them. The local police had been reinforced by eight members of the King's African Rifles. But so concerned were the authorities as to the possible reaction of the people to the arrests, it was decided that two platoons of the Royal Rhodesia Regiment – a white territorial unit – would march through the night to arrive at Nkhata Bay about 9.00am. For whatever reason, never explained, the reinforcements did not turn up until 3.00pm, and this delay had fatal consequences.

Everything had gone according to the plans of the authorities. The arrests were made at first light and the Congress activists were rounded up. When the M.V. Mpasa docked punctually at 6.30am, the prisoners were duly transported to the vessel and battened down in the hold. It was not long before word of the arrests filtered through the town and people began gathering in groups. As the numbers grew, they moved towards the prison calling for the release of their leaders. A sergeant of the Royal Rhodesia Rifles on the boat saw the people gathering and went ashore, allocating some of those under his control to guard duty at the post office and the local administration buildings. By now the large crowd of people had gathered outside the goal. The district commissioner came out to talk to them, but they would not be appeased. They wanted their leaders to be set free. The commissioner, realising that he had a very serious situation on his hands, made contact with the district commissioner in Mzuzu to find out when the military reinforcements were going to arrive, to discover that the Royal Rhodesia Rifles had not even reached Mzuzu. Explaining his situation to them, the authorities in Mzuzu agreed to send a platoon of the King's African Rifles to Nkhata Bay immediately.

When he returned to the streets, the district commissioner found an even larger, more angry, crowd. Word got out that the prisoners had been moved to the M.V. Mpasa and the people surged to the quay. There they faced four armed soldiers guarding the entrance. They faced each other for more than an hour without incident. Then very slowly the crowd moved forward forcing the soldiers back until they reached the point where the road opened onto the quay. At that point, the order was given to present the rifles to the crowd. The people were not intimidated and continued their slow, inexorable advance. The soldiers were told to stand at ease, and still the people came forward. The order to present arms and stand at ease was given twice more, but had no effect on the angry, determined population of Nhkata

Bay. The final order was given calling for independent fire; a few minutes later, the crowd scattered and forty Africans lay dead. A turning point had been reached.

In Britain, it was seen that there was no particular advantage in remaining in Nyasaland. It had no oil, copper, diamonds or gold to be exploited. By comparison with other colonies, the white population was quite small. Yet there seemed to be a wish among the white population to maintain a connection between the federated states. While Nyasaland was not blessed with natural mineral wealth, its migrant labour force was an important source of labour for the Rhodesias.

Opposition to colonial rule continued and the currents of change were flowing through the continent - many of the former colonies had achieved independence and others were well on the way to achieving it. On 1st April, 1960, Banda was released from prison. The state of emergency was lifted in June 1960 and by September of the same year the last of the political detainee, the ones considered to be the most danger to the colonial power, were released. These were Dunduza Chisiza and Harry Chimpembere.

Banda was now the leader of the Malawi Congress Party (formerly the Nyasaland African Congress). Other newly-independent countries in Africa had looked back to their history to re-name this entity of the nation-state, a troublesome legacy of European colonisation. The Gold Coast became Ghana, the Belgian Congo became Zaire. So, too, Hastings Kamuzu Banda looked to this history of the lake for the new identity of this country-in-the-making. The Maravi had come from Zaire and had settled in the northern part of the country, from where they spread out and eventually formed a powerful kingdom that covered much of present-day southern Malawi as well as parts of what is now Zambia and Mozambique. Though each clan or group was an independent settlement, they maintained a loose federation under a paramount chief and thus remained a powerful force. A Portuguese map of 1546 records the lake as Lake Maravi. 'Maravi' means flame, or light or rays in Chichewa. In Chichewa (one of two current official languages, the other being English) the letters 'r' and 'l' are interchangeable and the v is pronounced with a sound somewhere between v, w and f. So Maravi becomes Malawi and a powerful symbol of identity.

Glyn Jones was appointed as acting Governor in August 1960 (he was appointed Governor April 1961). His brief was to persuade Dr. Banda to accept a seat on the Executive Council before the proposed new constitution, which would give an African majority in both the legislature and the executive, so that he might see the internal workings of the federal system and come to accept it. Banda refused the offer of a seat, and refused any communication with the governments in the other federated states. He was invited by the Colonial Office to a constitutional conference held in London, where his demands for the dismantling of the Federation were as strong as ever. In the general elections held following the conference in 1961, the Malawi Congress Party won a large majority in the Nyasaland Legislative Council. He continued his total opposition to federation, demanding its dismantling at every opportunity. In February 1963 Nyasaland was granted internal self-government within the Federation and Hastings Kamuzu Banda became Prime Minister. The Governor, Glyn Jones, was still the Head of State. Eventually, in December, 1963, as the independence of other African counties continued apace, the Federation of Rhodesia and Nyasaland was finally abandoned, much to the delight of the African population in all three countries.

When secession from the Federation was completed in 1964, a general election was held almost immediately after which Dr. Banda and the Malawi Congress Party controlled the Assembly. In July 1964, independence from British colonial rule within the Commonwealth was achieved and Nyasaland was renamed Malawi. In 1966 Malawi was declared a republic and a single-party state. H.K. Banda became its president. In 1971 he had himself declared Life President.

— Chapter 5 —

Banda the dictator

For the Malawian people who had struggled under colonialism, independence offered the chance to re-connect with their own history and to re-forge a new identity for themselves. Unfortunately for them, they had exchanged one form of oppression for another, though few could have realised it at the time. For the more perceptive among them, signs of Banda's desire for absolute power had already been made visible to those nearest him. He had already demanded and received a free hand in choosing Party officers in 1958. He persisted in calling his cabinet colleagues, men of intellect and education, 'my boys'. In June, 1962 speaking in the legislative assembly, he said "We don't say, what do you want? What is it? It is what Kamuzu says goes over there."[1] One cannot help but get the impression that those who had invited Banda to take the helm of the Malawi Congress Party (formerly the Nyasaland African Congress) must have begun to have second thoughts and regret their messianic creation.

One of Banda's party colleagues, a brilliant young man, Dunduza Chisiza stated in the early 1960s that "One thing is clear, that no effort should be spared to prevent the establishment of a dictator. Salvation seems to lie not in cure but prevention."[2] Chisiza had been studying economics in Birmingham and had supported the return of Banda to Malawi. When Banda was elected President of the Malawi Congress Party in 1958, Chisiza was recalled from Britain and became Secretary General of the Party. He was imprisoned with Banda in Gwelo when the state of emergency was declared. During his detention, he spent his time working on the plans for Malawi's economic future. The fact that he was not released until six months after Banda indicates that the authorities were more concerned about the threat of Chisiza's abilities to organise opposition. When the country achieved self-government in 1961, Dunduza Chisiza became Parliamentary Secretary to the Ministry for Finance.

Chisiza was already contemplating the future of an independent Malawi. He obviously had deep concerns about the possibilities of dictatorships in newly-independent African countries generally. He was ideally placed to

---

[1] Lwanda, John Lloyd, Kamuzu Banda of Malawi: A study in promise, power and paralysis (Glasgow: Dudu Nsomba Publications, 1993) p 14.

[2] Ibid. p 36.

gauge H.K. Banda's personality, given his position in the Party and his detention with him in Gwelo. He wrote essays dealing with the themes of post-independence government vis-à-vis trade unions, the need to avoid the dangers of patronage and corruption in government, and relationships with western governments in order to obtain aid. He had concerns about the cult of the messianic leadership and its effects on government. He wrote "To a man who has been surrounded by submissive associates for a long time, the exercise of initiative by his associates is easily misconstrued as a sign of rivalry and disloyalty....the mind of a dictator is obviously not open to persuasion."[3] Harry Chimpembere had already seen signs of incipient despotism in Banda: "There was the temperament of Dr. Banda to consider. Whenever you criticised him, he flared up so violently that you had to consider your own position."[4]

Chisiza not only held strong views of the political development of Malawi, he was not afraid to articulate them in the public forum. He delivered his paper "The outlook for contemporary Africa" at the Nyasaland Economic Symposium in 1962. Banda had blatantly rejected many of the conclusions of this symposium. Dunduza Chisiza was killed in a car crash in 1962 only months after the symposium. He was only thirty-two years old. Not only had Malawi lost one of its brightest intellects, but Chisiza was to be the first of many people who disagreed with Banda and were to meet with sudden and unfortunate deaths.

There was great unease within the country following Chisiza's death, so much so that Yatuta Chisiza, brother of Dunduza, felt obliged to state publicly, in the legislative assembly, his loyalty to Banda. The speculation that Dunduza Chisiza's death was no accident was further fuelled by the appointment of John Tembo to the vacant post of Secretary of the Finance Ministry. For not only was he not qualified for the post, but he was an uncle of Cecilia Tamanda Kadzimira. Mama Kadzimira, as she became known, met Banda in 1958 when she, as one of a number of nurses, began working in his medical practice. She eventually became his secretary and finally his Official Hostess. The nature of the relationship can only be speculated upon, as any discussion of it became a detainable offence after independence. Members of Mama Kadzimira's extended family seemed to do quite well in obtaining government jobs and in Malawi's foreign service.[5] John Tembo was singularly successful in avoiding the fall-out of the many political

---

[3] *Ibid. p 35.*

[4] *Short, Philip, Banda (London: Routledge and Kegan Paul, 1974) p 200.*

[5] *Lwanda, op. cit. p 25.*

purges to occur during Banda's reign. John Tembo and Mama Kadzimira were a formidable pair.

By 1963, there were murmurings of discontent in the Malawi Congress Party. Many of the younger ministers in the cabinet were deeply concerned at Banda's increasingly authoritarian leadership. Not only did he call his cabinet colleagues 'my boys' but expected that they would behave like obedient children, always deferring to him. For the politicians, the death of Chisiza was still a fresh memory. There was also dissatisfaction that Banda had accepted a report that would give African workers lower wages than Europeans for doing the same work. There was disappointment at the slow rate of 'Africanisation'. There was deep concern at the decision to maintain political ties with South Africa. Another cause for concern was Banda's decision to introduce a hospital levy – a three-penny charge called a 'tickey'. Despite these many concerns, the cabinet did not voice its opinion. Perhaps the untimely death of Dunduza Chisiza urged caution. However, with Independence, the ministers summoned their courage and decided to tackle the issues of concern. Unfortunately, the lack of political nous on the part of the ministers meant that they made their move too soon and without sufficient planning.

The government was still enjoying its 'honeymoon' and the electorate was still euphoric at the achievement of independence from colonial rule. There had not been enough time to judge the worthiness of the new government or its leader. With their political energies expended on the goal of independence and their immersion in self-government, the young men had not built up a significant support for themselves within the government, with the members of parliament, nor in the wider arena of the country generally, particularly in the rural areas. The fact that Banda had instinctively understood the cult of the personality, built up a solid following, and always spoke rather deprecatingly of his ministers, meant that he was seen as the respected 'elder' who knew what was good for the country as a whole. Also, Chiume had done such a good job building up the messianic image of Banda before independence, that the people were hardly likely to listen to him and others telling them now that Banda was totally unsuitable for the office of Prime Minister.

Banda, politically astute as ever, had already set up a network of support both inside and outside the Party. The group of dissenting ministers did not present a united front, divided as they were among themselves on how to proceed. However, at a summit of the Organisation for African Unity held in Cairo, Chiume upstaged Banda. He had tried to persuade Banda to take a stronger line on the condemnation of Portuguese colonialism in

Mozambique. Banda was took grave exception to Chiume's comments. On their return to Malawi, Banda threw down the gauntlet to the disaffected in his cabinet with his 'one party, one leader, one government and no nonsense about it' speech given at the airport to those welcoming him home. He left all who listened in no doubt about his feelings: "You, the common people, are the real Malawi Congress Party. Watch everybody! Even Ministers – and I tell you when they are present, right here. Watch them, everybody! If they do what you do not think is good for the Malawi Congress Party, whether they are Ministers or not, come and tell me. It is your job to see that nothing injures or destroys the Party. Ministers are human beings, you know.... I am saying this because I know we have strange funny people here very soon. Ambassador for this country, Ambassador for that country, and they will be trying to corrupt people in the Party, and they will be starting with the Ministers and Members of the National Assembly. So, I want you to be vigilant. One Party, one leader, one government and no nonsense about it."[6] This had the effect of uniting all the ministers with the exception of John Tembo against him. Some days later, six of the ministers (neither Chiume nor Cameron were with them and Chimpembere was away in Canada at a conference on education) made a decision to meet with and challenge Banda. Switching tactics from aggression to dialogue, as the situation demanded, he managed to appease them and they left without achieving anything, other than forewarning the Prime Minister of their thinking.

Immediately after this, Banda sought to have preventative detention re-introduced. Colin Cameron, horrified that this rather crude tool of the colonial administration should be requested by a leader for use against his own people so soon after independence, felt obliged to resign in protest. This suited Banda's plans nicely, as it meant one less dissenting minister to worry about. For the disaffected ministers, meeting Banda without Harry Chimpembere was a significant misjudgement. Of all of them, he was the one with the most substantial following in the country. He was particularly popular with teachers and civil servants.

When the ministers had challenged him, Banda offered to resign, but they refused to accept his resignation. Perhaps fear of a backlash from the electorate was behind their refusal. Some commentators say that if they had accepted his resignation, given his cultural background, Banda would have felt unable to go back on his decision. Perhaps Banda knew exactly what he was doing in calling the ministers' bluff, and strengthened his hand as a consequence. A week later the ministers presented him with a list of their

---

[6] *Short, op. cit. pp 203-4.*

grievances. Being as politically inexperienced as they were, they gave Banda their list a full five days before the next cabinet meeting. They did all this without any consultation with Chipembere in Canada.

Their premature action gave Banda ample time to consolidate his support. There were plenty of ambitious men in the government anxiously waiting to step into the shoes of the ministers should they resign. On the day of the cabinet meeting, Banda was anything but conciliatory. He had no intention of resigning or holding talks with rebelling cabinet ministers. They, in turn, had decided to form an alternate government headed up by Orton Chirwa. This was the débâcle that greeted Harry Chipembere when he returned from Canada in early September 1964. He had no idea of what had gone on in government in his absence. Understanding only too well what was at stake, he attempted to heal the divisions between Banda and his ministers, but it was too late. In bullish mood, Banda received a unanimous vote of confidence from parliament on 10th September 1964. Not only that, he also received the support of the people, who perceived the ministers as upstarts, disloyal to the leader and hungry for power for themselves.

The free hand the committee of the Malawi Congress Party had given Banda was now used against them, as he suspended the remaining ministers, Chipembere, Chiume, Bwanausi, Msonthi, Chokani, Mkandawire, and Chirwa from cabinet. Colin Cameron had already resigned on principle. The governor, Glyn Jones, (who was still Head of State) attempted to set up a meeting to bring the ministers and Banda together, but Banda cancelled it. It is believed that he cancelled the meeting because of comments made by Harry Chipembere at a meeting in Mangochi. The *Nyasaland Times* quoted Chipembere as saying: "The present Malawi government is worse than Welensky's Federal Government... When we were elected we promised the people that all jobs being done by Europeans would be done by Africans. But Europeans who shot our people, burning their houses and ill-treating them, are still holding high posts in Zomba, Blantyre, Lilongwe and elsewhere."[7]

H.K. Banda now had the upper hand. He had the support of the government, the support of his newly-appointed, handpicked cabinet and most importantly, he had the support of the people of the country. Significantly, he also had the support of the governor who would have seen him as a uniting factor in the country. The dissenting ministers were divided among themselves and a number of them would have had more socialist leanings that would have left them suspect in the eyes of the British

---

[7] *Ibid. p 216.*

administration. Banda had also ingratiated himself with the white landowners and businessmen by appointing his former enemy, Michael Blackwood of the United Federal Party, to sensitive posts in trade and banking. (Blackwood had resolutely stood in the way of constitutional advance in the country during the Federation in the late 1950s).

Banda used his mass approval to purge the Malawi Congress Party of all suspected dissidents. Detentions were reinstated to silence any opposing voices. Many intellectuals were forced into exile. The country was stripped of all potential leaders and those who might initiate change. Hastings Kamuzu Banda, through skilful political manoeuvrings and manipulation of the masses, had become the all-powerful embodiment of Dunduza Chisiza's feared dictator.

* * * * *

Hastings Kamuzu Banda survived the cabinet crisis of 1964 and emerged stronger than ever. By silencing his opposition through detention and exile, and introducing a system of patronage to ensure the loyalty of those around him, he had a mandate to rule Malawi as he wished. His hand was further strengthened by international approval. As African countries became independent through the 1960s a new form of colonial influence was imposed, albeit in a less direct way than heretofore. The Cold War moved location from Europe to Africa, and that beleaguered continent, yet again, became the battleground for other nations' political rivalries.

Newly-emerging African governments were wooed by the main players in the Cold War. Countries were either pro-Western or pro-Communist (Chinese/Soviet), being financed and armed by each side, depending on their politics. Banda was very clearly pro-Western. He even went so far as to establish diplomatic relations with South Africa, despite the disapproval of other nations. Once in power, he eschewed the notion of a Pan-African movement, so beloved of his friend, Kwame Nkhruma and other new African leaders. His relationship with South Africa was greatly enhanced by its willingness to fund his dream of building a new capital city at Lilongwe when other western nations had refused to finance this project. Banda even allowed South Africa to use Malawi to give logistical support to the rebel Mozambican group RENAMO. This almost provoked a military crisis with Mozambique in 1986, which was only defused by the death of the Mozambican president Samora Michel, in a plane crash.[8]

---

[8] Carver, Richard. *Malawi: Between the referendum and the elections.* Writenet UK, May 1994

His relationship with South Africa and with Israel further benefited Banda when they trained his secret service. Banda built up a very efficient and utterly ruthless secret service. He would boast that the 'eyes of Kamuzu are everywhere.' The Malawi secret service was particularly adept at infiltrating opposition groups at home and abroad, limiting opportunity for any real opposition to develop. For those who attempted to challenge Banda's authority, the consequences could be, and usually were, devastating.

Another possible source of opposition to Banda was the trade union movement. Trade unions had been in existence from the 1940s onwards. Legislation allowing the formation and registration of trade unions was finally enacted in 1958. By independence in 1964, several trade unions had been formed. There was the Teachers' Union, the Transport and General Workers' Union, the Local Government Employees Union, the Commercial Workers Union, the Plantation and Agriculture Workers' Union, the Railway Workers' Union and the National Union of Mineworkers, which merged with the Building Construction Civil Engineering and Allied Workers Union.

Trade unionism had been fuelled by the injustices of colonialism. The fight for better wages and conditions became part of the fight for independence. In some cases, union leaders were also Malawi Congress Party members. In the period of self-government from 1961 to 1964, trade unions continued to flourish, so that by 1964 there were approximately nineteen trade unions in existence in Malawi. The trade unions affiliated to the Nyasaland Trade Union Council.[9]

From the beginning of self-government, it became clear that the interests of the Malawi Congress Party were diverging from those of the trade unions. There were two reasons for this. Firstly, the Malawi Congress Party had turned its attention to the economic development of Malawi and would not tolerate any disruption to that end; and secondly, trade union leadership was a potential source of challenge to Banda and the Malawi Congress Party hegemony. When strikes were threatened, the Malawi Congress Party-controlled government stepped in on the side of the employers, protecting their economic interests, and by extension, the economic interests of the government. These interventions effectively neutralised the power of the unions in their struggles with the employers.

Not surprisingly then, following the cabinet crisis of 1964, the state suspected that the unions sympathised with the dissident ministers. The government decided to force the unions to affiliate to the Party. Not only that, but the Malawi Congress Party would only co-operate with those

[9] Manda, Mtafu Almiton Zeleza. *The state and labour in Malawi.*
(Glasgow: Dudu Nsomba Publications, 2000) pp 22-30.

unions whose aims and objectives were acceptable to the Party. The trade unions had no choice in this matter – affiliation was mandatory. At least eleven unions were de-registered because their leaders disagreed with these new limitations. The Commercial Workers Union was de-registered twice, because the government stated that it lacked competent leadership – in other words, leadership that would not suit the Party. Another weapon in the government's attack on the trade unions was the practice of co-opting union leaders into the Party or the civil service. Cleverly, Banda did not officially outlaw trade unions, but the circumstances were such that unions were totally compromised as a force for change. Those union leaders not willing to be co-opted disappeared, met with unfortunate 'accidents' or chose exile.[10]

With each passing year, Banda's suffocating grip on Malawi tightened. In 1965 Harry Chipembere attempted a revolt, but it was poorly organised and put down quickly and severely. In 1966 Malawi became a de facto one-party state. All citizens were required to buy a Party card. Possession of a Party card was necessary for access to markets, to public transport, and even to hospital. There are stories of pregnant women being pressurised to buy a card for their unborn baby! Those who refused, on principle, to buy cards suffered severely. In 1967 Jehovah's Witnesses refused to buy the cards, thereby precipitating a number of pogroms against them. Members of their congregation were detained, others exiled, and very many were killed. In 1967 also, Yatuta Chizisa (brother of Dunduza) attempted another revolt, but it too failed. Anti-Banda Malawians were not even safe in exile. In 1979 Attati Mpakati, the leader of the Socialist League of Malawi, had almost all his fingers blown off in a parcel bomb attack. In 1983 he was found murdered in Harare, Zimbabwe.

In 1984, three senior government ministers and a member of parliament died in a car crash at Mwanza. They were Aaron Gadama, Minister for the Central Region and Leader of the House, Twaibu Sangala, Minister for Health, Dick Matenje, Secretary-General of the Malawi Congress Party and David Chiwanga the member of parliament for Chikwawa. In 1983, Dr. Banda had expressed an interest in going abroad for a year for a type of 'sabbatical'. There were moves afoot to nominate John Tembo, uncle of Mama Kadzimira as a caretaker president in Banda's absence. The four MPs were against this move, believing it to be a prelude to installing Tembo as President after Banda retired or died, and were vocal in their opposition. Shortly after their protest, they met with a car 'accident' at Mwanza, while driving home from a cabinet meeting. There is evidence that the men were

---

[10] *Ibid. pp 34-41*

shot. Despite orders from the police that the sealed coffins were not to be opened – a priest visiting the house of one of the deceased was shown the wounds by the deceased's sister. There was a bullet hole in each temple, and one in the forehead.

In 1989, a journalist, Mkwapatire Mhango, in exile for daring to criticise Banda's totalitarian leadership died with his whole family after his home in Lusaka, Zambia was fire-bombed. In 1981 Orton and Vera Chirwa, both respected lawyers, were kidnapped from Zambia, tried for treason and sentenced to death. The international outcry that their mockery of a trial evoked meant that their death sentences were commuted to life imprisonment. Both spent long periods in solitary confinement. Orton Chirwa died in prison in 1992. Vera Chirwa was eventually released on 24th January, 1993 after serving twelve years. Though they were held in the same prison, Vera and Orton Chirwa only had two opportunities to see each other. One occurred eight years into their sentence and the second in September 1992, when a delegation of British lawyers was allowed to meet the Chirwas. Orton Chirwa died soon after this.

In the first ten years of Banda's rule, the economic development of Malawi was quite impressive. Not blessed with great mineral wealth, the country's biggest asset was its agriculture. Banda concentrated on the development of agriculture. This policy was quite successful and ensured his popularity with the rural population, which accounted for about 80-85% of the total. None of the attempted revolts against Banda in the mid-1960s had the support of the rural population and were doomed to failure. By the late 1970s when the economic outlook began to look a lot less positive, Banda, had had more than ten years of autocratic rule to consolidate his position and make his positions as president and leader of the Malawi Congress Party invincible. His security was helped in no small way by the activities of the Malawi Young Pioneers and the Youth League.

The Young Pioneers and the Youth League formed a militia created by Banda and were independent of the police and army. They were young men and women between the ages of fifteen and twenty-five years. Young people who became members of this paramilitary force left school early and were taken to special training camps, where they received their training. To begin with, these training camps were set up and organised by the Israelis. The Young Pioneers wore distinctive red shirts; the Youth League wore green, and both were fiercely loyal to Banda. There were Young Pioneers or Youth League cadres in every village and every community, and they truly were 'the eyes of Kamuzu'. Even members of their own families felt constrained in their conversations in the presence of the Young Pioneers or the Youth League. It was not unusual for Young Pioneers or Youth League members to denounce a member of their own family to the authorities.

The Young Pioneers had originally been formed to go out and train the local people in the best agricultural methods and other development projects, and were successful in this, but very soon they became an integral part of Banda's machinery of oppression of the people of Malawi. They had the power of arrest and operated independently of the police force and army, answerable only to Banda.

The Young Pioneers and the Youth League may have been both the eyes and ears of Kamuzu, but in order to exert an iron grip on the country and extinguish any hope of dissent, Banda needed even more control. For him the two most obvious areas over which he needed to exert ultimate control were the judiciary and the press.

Until 1969, when they resigned, the four High Court judges in Malawi were British. Very quickly, it had become obvious that the courts were not to be allowed to function independently of the government. If Banda did not like the result of a particular judicial process, he had no compunction about overruling decisions made by the court. During the colonial period, traditional courts had been set up to deal with tribal disputes. Banda extended the role of these traditional courts to allow them to try murder cases and then further extended their role to include treason. So these courts operated parallel to the system inherited from the British. There was no right of appeal from the traditional court to the existing High Court. The type of crime of which the defendant was accused, or indeed the result desired by Banda, decided the system by which the unfortunate person was tried. The traditional courts had the power to impose the death penalty following trial, a power that it used many times.

The single radio station: the Malawi Broadcasting Corporation, and two newspapers, the *Daily Times* and the weekly *Malawi News*, were very tightly controlled by the government. There was no television station in Malawi during Banda's rule. From Independence in 1964, no opposing voice to Banda's was tolerated. Independent-minded journalists suffered considerably for their courage, even though they may have been very circumspect in their criticism. No dissension from the party line was allowed. Foreign journalists found it impossible to operate from a base within Malawi to report on events there. Those who tried found themselves expelled.

A Censorship Board was established in 1968 for mainly political rather than any moral reasons. At times, the censorship could be carried to ludicrous ends. While pornography was banned, certain medical text-books were also listed by the Censorship Board because the illustrations in them were considered indecent. An early Lonely Planet travel-guide *Africa on the cheap* was banned because it was critical of the Banda regime. Travellers who looked as if they were on low-budget holidays were stopped, and searched for this 'seditious' guide-book. Any who had it in their possession seldom got across the border with the book intact. It is said that Simon & Garfunkel's song 'Cecilia' was also banned at a time when Mama Kadzimira and Kamuzu Banda were not on the best of terms. The words of the song suggested that 'Cecilia' was breaking the man's heart, therefore it was considered to be politically sensitive!

While the extremes of the censorship laws were laughable, the impact on the writers of the country was not. Many of the country's finest writers had to leave. Others tried to be more circumspect, using the time-honoured application of metaphor to cloak the true meaning of the literature. This was not always successful, as the fine Malawian poet, Jack Mapanje discovered. He found himself incarcerated, without trial, without explanation, for more than three years. He was picked up by the police at his own house in 1987, and his family did not see him at all for the next twenty-two months. They were not even sure where he had been detained. Their enquiries of Mapanje's whereabouts were met with official indifference. Eventually, through the courage of a prison guard who transported messages written on tiny scraps of paper, Mapanje was able to make contact with the outside world through Fr. Pádraig Ó Máille, an Irish missionary priest, who was a friend and colleague.

Through the years of independent rule there have been many people who were detained and were never seen or heard of again. Malawi has its own unfortunate quota of 'los desaparecidos.'

Detention meant being arrested without notice, without explanation, without legal redress and held in a detention centre for an unspecified time. Conditions in the detention centres were horrendous and up to 1987 systematic torture was perpetrated on detainees, both men and women. This included everything from the use of weapons of torture on the body generally, through the use of electric shocks to, and the crushing of, the genital area, to sexual abuse by the insertion of implements or rape. While the torturers would in the main be men, women Malawi Young Pioneers were also involved in inflicting torture and degrading acts on the male detainees.

During all this time Banda was courted by the Western powers and considered by them to be a 'benevolent dictator' and a unifying force in the country. Through the efforts of Amnesty International in particular, the state-sponsored systematic torture was eventually halted, though the physical conditions within the detention centres were and continued to be appalling. A room measuring barely 3m x 3m, could contain twelve men in handcuffs and leg-irons. Sanitation comprised of one bucket. No exercise was allowed. The food consisted of meal and rotten vegetables - vegetables that would ordinarily be dumped. There was no doctor available to the detainees; if any medical assistance was required, it was administered by a paramedic. If there was any infringement of the prison rules, the detainee was stripped naked and thrown into a punishment cell. The cells had the equivalent of latter-day stocks, where the hands and feet of the detainee were chained to an iron rail embedded in the cell floor.

Detainees had no recourse to legal advice and were held at the president's pleasure. Martin Munthali was one of Banda's bodyguards during the fight for independence. During the cabinet crisis of 1964 he sided with the dissident ministers. After the failure of the ministers' action, he was charged and found guilty of possessing arms and was sentenced. When he finished his actual prison sentence, he was kept in detention at the president's pleasure until 1992. He was sixty-five when he was eventually released.

Detention also had implications for the extended family. If a person was detained, the finger of suspicion immediately fell on the whole family. People might find themselves dismissed from their employment, and shunned by their relatives, neighbours and friends. The fact that a detainee might be completely innocent had no bearing on the matter. To be linked, however peripherally, to a detainee was to be 'contaminated' oneself.

Ritual dancing formed an important expression of cultural identity for many of the tribal groups in Malawi. It was also an opportunity to form strong, united groups. Some of the traditional dances had strong military overtones in the choreography. After the unsuccessful Chimpembere revolt in 1965, members of some of the dance troupes found it necessary to burn their military-style uniforms, since being found in possession could, and did, lead to detention. Other opportunities for meeting were the bao groups. Bao was a skilled board game, and similar to chess. These bao groups were popular. Banda had realised the potential of these activities to become a source of opposition to his dictatorship, and lost no time in attacking and ridiculing the practices.

Apart from one or two notable exceptions, women in Malawi did not fare very well. While some of the ethnic groups in Malawi are matrilineal, they are not matriarchal. In fact, the various ethnic groups, whether patrilineal or matrilineal (the succession of males through the male or female line), were all strongly patriarchal. Dr. Banda capitalised on this cultural reality to successfully oppress women within the country. In Chewa society, (Kamuzu Banda was ethnically a Chewa), the leading male is *nkhoswe* (protector) of the females (*mbumba*) of his mother's line. Banda announced that he would be *nkhoswe* to the women of Malawi. As this idea of *nkhowse* had a very strong cultural meaning, it was cheerfully accepted by women initially. But the claim was mere rhetoric. Women had no status in the Banda dictatorship. When the Women's League was set up, any decisions of the women involved had to be ratified by the men at Party headquarters. Women could not achieve any significant level of authority within the Party. The district level was as high as they could go, and even then they were answerable to the District Chairman, who was always a man.[11]

In fact, Banda used the *nkhoswe* concept as yet another cleverly-designed weapon of 'divide and rule' manipulation. He warned men not to take women for granted or they could bring trouble on them. In strongly patriarchal societies where women have very little control over decisions that concern them and their lives, what little power they have they will use. As a result, suspicion and division was created within many families, with the men deeply suspicious of the women.

Banda's consuming need for admiration and adulation had implications for the women of Malawi. Wherever he went, he wanted spectacular dancing routines to be given by women. What had been a spontaneous and joyous action at political meetings in the early days carried out by both men and women, became an almost unbearable burden on women and their families. To begin with, the people had very little money, and clothes were not a priority with them. Food and education of the children were the primary concerns of most families. As a result, the women dancers were very poorly dressed. As they had to dance on demand, (the men were never forced) for Banda, he decided that they should have a uniform.

At first, each group just picked whatever material was available to them, but then Banda decided on material that was specially printed with his portrait. Since Banda was their *nkhowse*, the women presumed that they would be given a present of the material. They very soon realised that not only were they expected to buy this expensive material from their very limited resources, but Banda, their *nkhowse*, owned the company supplying it. In order to create a bigger market for his product, Banda decided that each of the twenty-four districts in the country should have a different material. If a woman moved to a different district, she was obliged to buy the material for that district. If there was a particular memorial or jubilee

---

[11] *Mkamanga, Emily, Suffering in Silence: Malawi women's 30 year dance with Dr. Banda (Glasgow: Dudu Nsomba Publications, 2000) p 33.*

celebration, new material was produced for that event and the women were obliged to buy it. Not to do so was to show disrespect for 'Ngwasi' (conqueror) and, by now, everybody knew the consequences of lack of respect for His Excellency, the Ngwasi, Life President, H.K. Banda.

On one occasion, some Asian traders, resident in the country, brought in material printed with generic portraits of both men and women. It had been manufactured in Japan for distribution in the African market generally. This material was immediately prohibited by Banda and importers had to destroy hundreds of bales of stock. Some traders were even expelled from the country for daring to import it in the first place. Many of the women who had bought the alternative material decided to burn it for fear that they would be accused of disrespect; some felt brave enough to take the chance of using it as bed linen. For some women the 'Banda' cloth comprised her best clothes, yet there were severe restrictions on wearing it. For instance, a woman could not use it to carry her baby, or wear it to any event other than church or Malawi Congress Party functions. When making the uniform, the portrait could not be positioned where it might be sat upon by the wearer. If a tailor committed the crime of cutting through the Banda portrait, he risked being detained.

While the women may have danced for Banda, and their performance a breathtaking spectacle, for many it was a dance of fear, of shame, a necessary evil to bear in order to protect themselves and their families from the reality of detention. For many knew the awful truth that detention was a fate worse than death.

President Banda appeared to be singularly skilled in dealing with any potential opposition. Those he could manipulate through patronage, he did. Those he could not manipulate, he terrorised. Those who could not be terrorised he had killed.

— Chapter 6 —
A call to missionary life

In 1965, around the time Harry Chimpembere was making his doomed bid to unseat Dr. Banda, over on the far western lip of Europe, a young Irish man was making a decision that was to set him on a slowly converging course with Hastings Kamuzu Banda and his government. When he decided that he would study for the priesthood, John Roche could not have imagined that it would lead him to the point where he would have to accept that he might have to pay the ultimate price for his faith.

The fifth of six children, John Roche had, in all respects, a conventional childhood in the Irish midland town of Athlone where he was born on 19th July, 1947. His father, Jack Roche, worked on the railway and his mother, Madge (née Kilroy), worked in the home, raising their five sons and only daughter. Exposed to the religious observances that were an integral part of Ireland of the 1950s and 1960s, John was attracted to the practice of faith. There was the daily prayer of the Rosary at home; serving at mass in his local parish of St. Mary's and singing in the church choir. He was a solid, steady youth, a good team player, not likely to lead the charge, but always there in support. Nothing marked him out as a likely candidate to be embroiled in the internal political affairs of a small country thousands of miles away.

Priests were not a strange presence in the Roche household to be brought into the parlour and fed from the best china. With two cousins on his father's side and one on his mother's, John was used to seeing priests as part of the extended family. So, it is not surprising then, that the idea of priesthood as a way of living, was integrated into John's thinking from an early age. Right up until the end of primary school the idea of being a priest was uppermost in his mind. After his primary schooling, there was a suggestion from some of the cousins that John might attend boarding school, but appreciating the importance to a child of growing to adulthood within a family, Madge Roche refused to send her son away to school. Instead, John attended the local Marist Brothers' secondary school.

As he set out on the new adventure of secondary school, all thoughts of a priestly vocation evaporated. John settled into life in secondary school with the same equanimity as he had come through primary school. Academic work did not pose any particular difficulties, and he soon discovered that he had a particular talent for football, which ensured popularity with both teachers and students. Secondary school proved as uneventful as primary school had been. By now, of course, girls had also been discovered and all the usual awkwardness, pain and pleasure of dating was part of John's teenage years.

By the beginning of the last year of secondary school, John Roche still had no idea of what he would like to do when he left school, nor was he unduly troubled by the fact. Ideas of being a footballer blended with others of being a train driver, or being a musician. In the spring term of 1965, a priest, Fr. Liam McSorley, from St. Patrick's Missionary Society, Kiltegan, Co. Wicklow, called to the Marist secondary school in Athlone. He spoke passionately to the final year students about his experience of priesthood and the great possibilities of foreign missionary work, particularly in Africa. He was a charismatic, enthusiastic priest and was able to communicate the source of his enthusiasm with conviction. McSorley struck a chord with John, who for the first time in almost five years began to reconsider the possibilities of priesthood. When he finished his talk Fr. McSorley told the young men where he would be if anyone wished to speak to him, and quietly retired to an office, to await inquiry. He did not impose on the boys or try to apply pressure in any way. He spoke from his conviction and then waited to see if it would bear fruit. Feeling the re-emergence of the possibility of priesthood as a future, John collected the application forms from Liam McSorley, admitting that he was not sure about the idea, as he thought it had long gone. McSorley's advice was to listen to the inner voice and give the idea some room. He explained that later in the year, near Easter, there would be a weekend in Kiltegan for prospective students, without any obligation, to give them a sense of the place.

The 'taste-and-see' weekend was a success. Located in the Wicklow Mountains, near the little village of Kiltegan, the mother-house of St. Patrick's Missionary Society offered a completely different landscape to the flat land of wide horizons in the midlands. The people John met there seemed warm and friendly and the atmosphere was welcoming. First impressions were good. Nevertheless, decisions were not easily made, and the struggle with the recognition of a priestly vocation was to continue right through until the Leaving Certificate examination and beyond, as constant and as irritating as a stone in a shoe. Eventually by the end of the summer of 1965, John decided that he would have no peace until he at least tried out the possibility, and so packed his bags and headed for the seminary.

The first year in the seminary was a spiritual year – a year of discernment. None of the seminarians went home to families during that year. For John this posed no problem and he entered into the rhythm of the year without any difficulty. Taking the year very seriously, he started the journey of prayer and getting to know God on a personal basis. It meant a re-visioning of God from the omnipotent deity, judging us sternly, to understanding God in Jesus as a real friend and companion on the journey of faith. While used to regular prayer within the family, this new perspective was a deepening of the whole experience.

At the end of this first, spiritual year, there was a period of discernment and reflection. There was discernment on the part of the student: was he really being called to this life, and on the part of the Society: did they think that he was really a suitable candidate for the priesthood and community and all that that would involve. For a small number the answer was 'no'. For the majority of students including John Roche, the answer was 'yes' on both sides.

In the second year of training, the students went to study at the Society's house of philosophy in Douglas, Cork. Philosophy was an exciting adventure – the mechanics of thinking, of logic, of epistemology. In the delight of interesting studies and camaraderie, the first year passed quickly. With the second year of philosophy studies came the first shocks. The starting number of thirty-two young men in the autumn of 1965, only dropped by one or two at the end of the first year. Nobody left during the second year and heading into the third year of training (second year of philosophy studies), people were suddenly disappearing overnight. Every month saw someone leaving. They went either late at night or very early in the morning, without notice, without any contact. It was a very unsettling time for the remaining students, as there was no opportunity for a leaving-taking or to understand why anyone decided to leave. Friendships had formed over the two years and more, and just to receive a cold, factual announcement that somebody was gone without saying goodbye, left a wound in the group. This was only just post-Vatican II, and the old ways still prevailed. Seven students left during the second year in Cork. Inevitably, this led to soul-searching for the remaining students, and a real questioning if they wanted to continue. The answer for most, including John, was a hesitant but open 'yes'.

After their philosophy studies, the students returned to Kiltegan for theology. In his second year of theology, about half way through his fifth year of seminary life, John faced a crisis of vocation. All along he had kept his interest in football, and it had grown to playing at club, college and county level and by now he was travelling to games every weekend. Academic work, which had been interesting and manageable, now became a chore. Prayer, which had always been a joy, now became a struggle. Having grappled alone for many months with the growing doubt about priesthood, John eventually went to his spiritual director. Listening carefully to the young man's difficulties, the spiritual director pointed out that among his problems was John's commitment to football. The stress of playing at three different levels of competitive football at the same time was taking its toll in physical exhaustion and his availability to the process of his priestly formation. Something had to give. For John, the idea of abandoning football was unthinkable, so a compromise was worked out. He was to cut back on his sporting commitment for two months. If at the end of the two months, he still felt that he wanted to leave, then that would be accepted without further argument. The uncertainty was added to by the constant trickle of those who discerned that they did not feel called to the priesthood after all and parted company with the Society. While for the class of '65 the biggest exodus was in the third year of seminary life, people left all through the whole training period of seven years.

During the two-months' grace, it became increasingly clear that physical exhaustion had been the main reason for the problem with studies and prayer. As the football commitment lessened, the world regained its equilibrium and John decided to continue. However, uncertainty had not been completely banished, but he held onto the words of his spiritual director 'none of us is sure' and things continued to improve. By the end of the third year of theology he felt ready for ordination. Of the thirty-two eager school-leavers who joined in 1965, eleven presented for ordination in 1972. Even in the final week before ordination a lot of soul-searching went on. The excitement of finally reaching the goal was balanced by the enormity of the commitment that at times weighed heavily on the students' hearts and minds. There were long hours of wakefulness on the night before ordination.

Newly-ordained and ready to plunge into any task, John looked towards South America. Post-Vatican II, the church in South America was blossoming under the development of liberation theology. There were endless possibilities for a young, strong and enthusiastic priest. However, other plans were being made for his destiny. John was asked to join the St. Patrick's Society mission in Malawi. It had only begun in 1970 and needed manpower for further development. Consulting an atlas and encyclopaedia, it was the expanse of Lake Malawi that first caught John's eye, tucked between Zambia on the west and Mozambique on the east. Malawi was a small narrow country of 45,560 square miles, one-third of which was water, leaving a land area of around 30,000 square miles, a little smaller than Ireland. While it did not have quite the romance of Brazil and Helder Càmara, Malawi beckoned.

The first difficulty was obtaining a work permit. The weeks dragged into months. August passed, September passed. John found himself kicking over the traces, anxious to get going. After seven years of study, anywhere on the face of the earth would do. South America began to heave into view again. Then in October 1972, the work permit was granted. Malawi was the mission.

* * * * *

En route to Malawi, there was a stopover in Nairobi, Kenya. For a young man from the peatlands of the Irish midlands, Kenya was a paradise. Apart from some time spent in Kent, England working with children from broken homes, in the last two summers of his training, John Roche had never left Ireland. The most noticeable flower on the trees at home were the white and red 'candles' of the horse chestnut, or the rich pink of cherry blossom; here the spectacular bluebell flower of the jacarandas of Nairobi looked like something left over from Eden. The heat and the sunshine were also a pleasant change from the dull October weather left behind. While here, there was enough time for a little sight-seeing, and the flamingos on Lake Nakuru added to the sense of magic of Kenya. The flamingos were not immediately distinguishable at first, appearing to be nothing more than a pink haze over the lake, but when they moved, the stories brought home by returned missionaries suddenly became real.

Taking leave of those who had flown with him as far as Kenya, John flew on alone to Malawi. Stepping off the aeroplane at Blantyre, the commercial capital, at around 8.00pm the first experience was the incredible heat. The heat of Nairobi had been a pleasant dry heat. This moist heat was like a physical enfolding presence. It prompted the thought, if it could be as warm as this at night, what on earth were the daytime temperatures likely to be. The airport officials were very competent, efficient and friendly without being invasive. The formalities of entry were completed without a hitch.

Sitting in his hotel room, with a magnificent 'flame of the forest' tree outside his window for company, John suddenly felt incredibly and powerfully alone. Here he was in a strange country where he knew nobody and at the start of a journey whose destination nobody could predict. Sitting in the centre of this loneliness, he suddenly remembered that he had been given a contact phone number. Searching it out, his heart lifted at the thought of company. A friendly male voice answered the phone and promised that as soon as his wife returned with the car, they would come over. In Malawi with an Irish construction company, Pat Power had heard of the likelihood of a new arrival and was expecting the call. He and his wife Kathleen came over to the hotel and provided a few hours of company and distraction and eased the overwhelming sense of loneliness.

Early next morning there was a flight on a 50-seater aircraft to Lilongwe to connect with the flight to Mzuzu. The onward flight to Mzuzu was in a tiny 6-seater aircraft and was anything but pleasant. But when Lake Malawi came into view in all its spectacular glory, the queasiness of the bumpy plane ride was forgotten. None of the reading about it could replace the breathtaking beauty of the immense lake shimmering in the morning sun as if spread out in welcome. Before too long the aeroplane throttled back and John was rather dismayed not to see anything that resembled an airport. Suddenly an earthen runway came into view with a little building, not more than a hut, off to one side. The plane lined up with the strip and touched down safely, covering everything and everyone in red dust. The powerful tang of hot earth greeted the travellers as they disembarked. As at Blantyre, the staff at the airport building was efficient, friendly and helpful. When all formalities were dealt with, it was off to the bishop's house at Katoto in the company of the small welcoming party that had been waiting.

Some of the priests and sisters waiting at Mzuzu seemed to be a little surprised at the longish mop of wavy hair sported by this raw young priest. The guitar slung over his shoulder added to the slightly 'hippie' look. The conservatism of these people was a little disconcerting. What was even more disconcerting was the order of one of his own confrères to get his hair cut. He cut through John's argument with the flat statement that 'Kamuzu does not allow long hair, so you get your hair cut immediately.' To the question 'Who is Kamuzu to tell me about my hair?' he received the sharp reply, 'Kamuzu is everything here!' This did not sound like the 'benevolent dictator' that was described in the books. As the days went on and he moved about the parishes waiting for his language classes to start, John became ever more conscious of the Party. The Party was everything: the Party demands this, the Party doesn't allow that. Always the Party. The first sense of unease was beginning to descend. It was heightened by the comment of an older, experienced priest when John noticed young people in red shirts around the place. He was told that they were the Malawi Young Pioneers, and 'to be very careful of them.' The sense of a very tightly-controlled society was beginning to impinge on John's consciousness.

Not being a talented student of language at school, John was a little concerned about the difficulties of learning the local language. The worries were in no way alleviated on hearing that language course was to be delayed for a couple of weeks because another St. Patrick's Society priest, Fr. Tom Leahy, was expected. However, the delay allowed time to see the northern part of the diocese and get a sense of the country. The overwhelming sense was of the sheer physical beauty of the northern province. The open grasslands of the Nyika Plateau contained a wide variety of plant and bird life. The escarpment from Rumphi down to the lake offered splendid views. While many of the roads were dirt roads, the sheer beauty of the surroundings made travel worthwhile.

After two weeks, Fr. Tom Leahy arrived, as did the opportunity to learn Chitumbuka and begin to communicate at some meaningful level with the people. Prior to this, the inability to communicate was having a depressing effect. Sunday, without the football of the previous four or five years, was a very long day indeed. Sunday newspapers did not exist. There was just one paper during the week, the *Malawi Times*, and a weekly paper on a Saturday, *Boma Lathu*, (The Government Gazette). Without the local language, John could not even help out in any meaningful way with mass.

A month was spent in Katete at the southern end of the diocese with Fr. Wolfer, a French priest. He gave some hours of instruction to the class, then the students spent time by themselves practising. There were about eight people in the language class already learning the language. They were about three weeks ahead of the two new arrivals, but this helped the beginners and good fun was had by all in the evenings. Fr. Wolfer then arranged for some of the local people to come in for practice in conversation. Though good progress was made, both John and his fellow-student knew that the only way to come to grips with the language was to go and live in a village with the people. This had not been tried before, but Fr. Wolfer was open to the idea and it was arranged for the two men to live with a village community for a month. They lived completely as the community lived, apart from having clean drinking water delivered to them once a week from the nearest mission.

In the early days communication with the villagers was mainly by sign language. Then as knowledge and confidence grew, they became more proficient in speaking. The villagers took the two awkward, stuttering men to their hearts immediately. They were given a grass-roofed hut for themselves. They ate with the community, worked with the community and prayed with the community. The children were fascinated with John and his fellow-priest. They used run their hands up and down the arms of these strange white hairy creatures, and collapse in laughter at the absurdity of it. The children were particularly helpful in making conversation and offered correction when necessary, but correction in the gentlest, most civilised way. If John said something incorrectly, the child would gently repeat it in the correct way. There was no ridicule. The children were wonderful and valued and cherished by all the community. They were appreciated for themselves and allowed to experiment, make mistakes, to rejoice, in short, they were allowed the freedom to be children.

While there were individual families in the village, the village itself was one big extended family. The men ate together, the women ate together and the children ate together. Only when the children were grown men and women did they join the adult groups. The group identity was very strong. A person would very seldom be left alone.

Every morning the village came alive at cockcrow. The day started with community prayer. Then there was work to be done in individual family gardens. The gardens were fields of about two acres and supplied the families' needs, with a little over for selling on if they were lucky. Any spare cash went towards the education of the children. It was the priority of the family that the children would receive the best education they could afford. If the gardens did not need attention, there might be hunting in the forest. Or, it might be time for chatting. Chatting is very much part of the African fabric of life. It forms relationships, sustains them and helps to resolve difficulties with the minimum of disruption. Individual needs are realised in and through the community.

Football was a source of great excitement and fun. The two priests had brought a football with them, and many matches were played, though the stamina of the white men collapsed after only a half-hour or so in the heat. Attempts to introduce gaelic football failed miserably, soccer being the game of choice of the young men of the village.

Bed-time came early, around 9.00pm, as there was no electricity. Necessary light was supplied by a little tilly lamp. When darkness fell, it was the time for storytelling. Much of the wisdom of the tribe is contained in the canon of stories and proverbs that are repeated through the generations.

Breakfast was a maize meal the villagers called porridge, though it looked more like semolina. Prodigious quantities of the stuff were laid in the centre of the table. It was hard to believe that ten men would be able to get through it. But they did. The main meal was boiled maize. The kernels were taken from the cob, pounded and boiled. It might have the addition of a few greens. Meat was a luxury. Occasionally, a chicken would be killed because of the visitors. Sometimes meat was brought out from the mission, but it would have to be cooked immediately as there was no refrigeration. The evening meal was even more mountains of cooked maize. From time to time there were little delicacies. If it rained, flying ants came to the surface, these were cooked and offered to the two men. But their courage failed at the sight of them. Eventually before he left, John was persuaded to try them. The woman who offered them explained that they were already cooked, but that she would roast them, which might make them more appealing. He ate them and had to admit that they were not too bad.

While the food was monotonous and bland, it was plentiful and the people looked strong and nourished. The biggest problem for them was the lack of transport if things did go wrong. Even though the village was on high land and was not known as a malarial area, the period between October and Christmas was the peak time for the disease and people did fall ill. It was about 25 km to the dispensary to get medication. One evening, the villagers were trying to prop a very sick man on a bicycle to bring him for badly-needed medical help. Another time, a pregnant woman in difficulties had to be transported in the same way. The ox and cart were just beginning to come into the village at that time. The money for these was provided by sons who went to work in the mines of South Africa. Migrant labour was the only source of hard cash for the families.

It was part of growing up for men that they go and work in the mines of South Africa. They married young, during March or April, left their wives pregnant and went off to work in the mines. The cash they sent home allowed the families to buy oxen and carts, or farm implements such as ploughs. At this time, the government was pursuing a strong agricultural policy, encouraging the people to work the land. With the cash supplied by the migrant labourers, this became possible.

The next hurdle for John in settling in to his new home, was Christmas. In Ireland, Christmas was particularly about linking up with old friends. Here in Mzuzu, on Christmas Eve there was no chance of walking down the street in the late afternoon and bumping into an old school friend, or an old football buddy. Everything was different. There was no commercial build-up, no street decorations or street lighting. People's concerns were around the real meaning of the Christmas celebration: whether or not they would have a priest to celebrate mass; how the community might celebrate the occasion. But just before Christmas an event occurred that was to lodge in his mind and be part of John's thinking. He went into a shop and found a young white woman of about eighteen or nineteen years of age, kneeling down and totally embarrassed. Over her stood two Young Pioneers, both men (the YP also recruits young women), and they were yelling at this young woman and berating her because her dress was too short. They told her that the dress should reach the ground. The law said it must reach the ground. One of the Young Pioneers took a scissors and started to cut the hem to lower the dress. The other people in the shop were laughing, partly in relief that this time it was someone else that this was happening to and not to them. Watching the young woman's humiliation and not saying anything in her defence profoundly affected John. He was barely two months in the country and he knew that he could not interfere in the affairs of the Young Pioneers. Stories abounded of expatriates expelled for what appeared to be minor infractions of the law. Yet he was filled with shame at his silence.

At Christmas, the Medical Missionaries of Mary who ran St. John's hospital nearby invited John and others to a round of carol-singing at the homes of the medical personnel on Christmas Eve. To be part of something familiar, even if it was many degrees warmer than home, meant a lot. After the Christmas Day masses, the sisters put on a meal in the evening and invited all the local priests. The day ended happily and a major hurdle had been overcome.

After Christmas and their time in the village, the two language students took their leave. Living in the village and learning the language suddenly gave purpose and meaning to this whole new venture of mission in a foreign land. For John Roche, it meant connecting to the people, connecting to the culture, connecting to the country in a very real way. Even the climate in the higher lands of the north was more pleasant than expected. The future could be contemplated with a significant degree of optimism.

—— Chapter 7 ——
Nkhamenya

Early in 1973, John was assigned to his first parish, Nkhamenya, in the most southerly part of the northern diocese of Mzuzu, where he lived with two Dutch priests, Fr. P. Nuyens and Fr. J. Kocken, both members of the Missionaries of Africa. The compound also included religious sisters and represented a truly international community where conversations about gaelic football and Irish politics really did not have a place. Nkhamenya was the largest parish in the diocese with about 30,000 Catholics. The model of church discovered here was an enlightening experience for John. He wondered many times what the Irish church would be like if its lay members were encouraged to be as involved as they were in Malawi. Because of the shortage of priests, mass was only celebrated once a month in some of the villages and outstations. On the other Sundays, lay leaders lead a prayer service.

Having arrived only eight years after independence, there was some difficulty in trying to get to know the parishioners. While they were most gracious in their welcome of the new priest, because it meant that they could receive the sacraments, administratively the white man still represented authority. A person went to his office if there was a problem but the white man was not somebody who was invited into the home of a Malawian. The white person had represented oppression and racist attitudes, placing little or no value on the worth of the African. A certain amount of unease remained around the relationship even after independence. It was even part of the language: the white man was usually called Bwana, meaning boss or master. Conscious that he was the outsider, and mindful of the generous welcome he received, John found himself again and again trying to prevent use of this honorific. Eventually, he spoke from the altar and asked the congregation to call him John, or father or brother or companion, or anything at all they deemed suitable, but not to call him Bwana. However, John fared better than many of the other European priests, being Irish. The Malawians could identify a little more readily with the Irish person. There were many similarities in the colonial histories of the two countries. Also the Irish 'elastic' attitude to time was more in keeping with the African concept, and both the Irish and Malawians loved to chat. Despite their inclination to chat, forming anything other than superficial friendships under the political conditions that existed in Malawi was almost impossible. Compliance with the Party rules invaded all aspects of life and no criticism, no matter how mild or circumspect, was tolerated. Friendship with foreigners meant risk. So, despite huge goodwill towards the church and great voluntary commitment to it, the all-pervading fear meant that trust could never be allowed to develop.

Politically, Nkhamenya was a sensitive parish, for though it was in the northern diocese, it was located in the central region, H.K. Banda's home territory. The main support for the Malawi Congress Party (MCP) was also in the central region. Banda viewed the north with great suspicion and given the linguistic and cultural differences between the north and the rest of the country, tensions were never very far away. One time the parish built a church at one of its outstations. When the church was built, the parish heard that a relative of the president had bought about 200 acres of land around the church. The truth was more likely to be that he had just appropriated the land. All the villagers on the land were told to move. There was no alternative housing provided for them. They were just given a date and told to be gone from the land. Concerned about the grave injustice being perpetrated on the villagers, John started talking to people to find out what could be done. He tried to find out where representations might be made. He was told again and again that the relative of the president could do whatever he liked. Some representatives of the community went to a local politician about it, but he just told them to pack their bags and go, as per the directive. The parish held onto the church, but in the end the landowner just took it over as a storage facility. The church ceased to function. It had no community, its congregation had been made to disappear.

Again, there was the challenge to the young missionary priest: how was the gospel message of justice being preached through the acceptance of such treatment meted out to the villagers? Discussions with fellow priests reached no satisfactory conclusion. The best that could be said was that in order to help the people, accommodation with the oppressive regime had to be achieved. It was an uneasy accommodation, liable to disruption at any time, as happened when one group of catechumens was making the final preparation for baptism. The president was to pass through the area on the next day. The Party officials insisted that all liturgical preparations be halted and everybody in the mission, about 400–500 people in all, were ordered to be on the roadside by 6.00am in preparation for the president to pass through at about 2.00pm. The parish priest made representations to the Party officials, explaining what was going on, and promising that everybody would be in place by 11.00am, still in plenty of time for the Presidential cavalcade. Risking being listed as a Prohibited Immigrant (P.I.), he pressed the issue. In the end, he was forced to concede. The wishes and desires of the Party were paramount. Resistance was not acceptable and could have very severe consequences.

Possible Party reaction had to be factored into every situation. While still in Nkhamenya, John was manager of the Catholic schools in the parish. The main school in the mission was having problems with its headmaster and parents were very concerned. There was a very talented and able man working in a smaller rural school who would be better suited to the main mission school. Meetings with both school boards were convened and while the small school was upset at the loss of their headmaster, they accepted the importance of a well-run larger school at the central mission. The local ministry had sanctioned the move and the transfer was organised. All seemed to run smoothly until the day a large ministerial car drew up outside one of the outstations where John was working. Mr. Aaron Gadama, the Regional Minister of the central region stepped out, walked over to the small house, and with few formalities, told John that the order to transfer the new headmaster had to be rescinded immediately, and the re-appointment of the original headmaster was to follow.

Up to now, John had obeyed the instruction to keep his head down and get on with his work and to ignore the provocation of the Party machine. This most recent intervention was more than he could bear. He demanded to know the reason for the interference in the school appointment. He was told that the Party wanted the appointments reversed. Committed now to confrontation, he replied that such a reason was insufficient. All the correct procedures had been adopted. The transfer was to stand. Mr. Gadama became quite angry and made it very clear as he departed that this refusal would have consequences. Too angry to feel threatened, John went back to the central mission to report on his confrontation. His parish priest was very supportive, but then word came summoning John to the bishop's house in Mzuzu. John's humour had not improved over the 200-mile trip and he was none too pleased to hear his bishop telling him that he must accede to the Party's request, that there were other more important things to consider. Having kept silent for over two years on many issues of injustice, John was in no mood to be in any way conciliatory. For him, this was an extremely important issue, not only for the principle involved, but also for the reality of good education for the children.

John ended up in confrontation with his bishop and refused to rescind the order transferring the new headmaster. He also refused to have anything to do with physically transferring the two men back to their original locations. The bishop stepped in and organised transport for the exchange. John was left seething with anger, and feeling totally impotent in face of the Party wishes and the Church's ready compliance. Though all proper procedures had been observed, though lengthy dialogue had taken place with all the people involved, in the end nothing mattered except the desires of the Party. That the Church leadership should bow to the pressure of the Party only added to the feelings of anger and helplessness and was to lead to a sense of betrayal. This was to be the pattern over the succeeding years. In their attempts to operate in a climate of dignity and respect for all, and also out of a real and justifiable fear, the church leaders very often appeared to be co-operating with the Party. The gospel message of justice, peace and truth was smothered by the all-pervading fear of the Party. There was very real fear around any questioning of the Party's methods. Yet the people continued to live, work and rear their families; they learned not to question the calamities that befell them. Their acceptance of their lot and working within the parameters of that was a powerful lesson to the angry young man.

The spirit of the people was slowly being choked, yet they struggled to remain alive. Their main expression of creativity was in religious ways. The most overt creativity in the early to mid-1970s was centred on liturgy, where there was dance, music, song, bible translations and depiction of bible stories. Music and song were performed very guardedly. Poetry was written in metaphor. Nothing could be explicit. Malawi Young Pioneers were everywhere – the eyes and ears of the Party - and nobody wanted to risk their wrath. Somebody could just disappear without warning or be beaten up for saying something the Party did not like. Even when the Party 'invited' comment, it was not safe to do so. At one time, Chief Phiri, a chief in Nkhamenya spoke up at a Malawi Congress Party Meeting. The president had encouraged such participation, by telling the participants to feel free to comment. The chief spoke up about worries about the state of the country. He was taken, beaten and had his chieftainship removed from him and given to somebody who was not in line for inheritance.

Fear and suspicion abounded. It was safer to say nothing at all. Nobody knew who was listening. For very little reason, people would be severely beaten, or taken away. If somebody was detained, the whole family fell under suspicion, and even members of the extended family risked losing their jobs and social exclusion: if you associated with a family under suspicion, you too then fell under suspicion. That the detainee may have done nothing other than make an unguarded remark was totally irrelevant.

There is the story of a government security chief who was detained in 1976 because it was alleged that he was plotting a revolt against the government. His wife and family were placed under house arrest in Blantyre. Concerned that her mother-in-law should know what happened, the wife smuggled a letter out through a servant. The eighty-year-old mother-in-law could not believe this was happening to her son, and decided to travel to Blantyre to check on the family. Having waited a long time for the bus, she got an opportunity of a lift with a man in an old pick-up truck. Before long they met a roadblock. (Police roadblocks were common). When asked her business by the police, she told them the whole story, even to showing them the letter from her daughter-in-law. As her son-in-law had such a senior government position, she fully believed that the police were going to help her. The elderly lady was detained for being the mother of a detainee. The driver of the truck who had no family connection, and had given the lady a lift out of kindness, was also detained for his association with a relative of a detainee. Both spent six years in detention. When she eventually returned home, the old woman discovered that her husband had been beaten to death by members of the Youth League and their house had been burned down.[1] So fear of the Party, of the police, particularly of the Malawi Young Pioneers and Youth League, meant there was no opportunity for discussion and certainly no dissent.

Despite the weight of oppression, or perhaps because of it, the Church in Malawi was a very inclusive church with a high degree of participation by the lay members. In the early seventies, concomitant with liberation theology in other parts of the world, was the idea of the Basic Christian Community. Bishop Kalilombe of Lilongwe was the pioneer of the movement in Malawi, and had written extensively about the concept. Because of the distances to be covered and the lack of easy transportation for the people, many communities only had mass celebrated for them once a month. In the central mission at Nkhamenya there were three priests, one religious sister and a number of catechists. They looked after an area of about sixty to seventy miles in extent. When mass was not available for a community, they themselves organised a prayer service with scripture and prayer. Coming from Ireland in 1972, this amount of lay involvement in Church was an eye-opener for John and a vision as to how things should be done. It was a pastoral priority of the mission to facilitate that commitment and participation by the lay Church, so there was particular emphasis placed upon leadership training and formation of the people. Local people took

[1] *Mkamanga, Emily, Suffering in Silence: Malawi women's 30 year dance with Dr. Banda. p58*

ownership of their Church. While there was input from, and consultation with, the religious leaders, in the final analysis the people articulated the vision of Church and took decisions in dialogue with each other. Within the basic Christian community, everything was discussed. Discussion was not just on matters of worship and ritual, it encompassed social issues affecting the group, and from that certain projects would be initiated, for example on matters of health. The commitment of young people in the Church was very strong. Once they saw care and concern for them, they responded with interest and leadership.

Those Catholics in the Malawi Young Pioneers were very much part of the Christian communities in the earlier years and would not have seen any conflict between their faith and their political ideology. It was not unusual if the Party was having a meeting of any sort to invite a representative of one the local churches to open the proceedings with a prayer. If there were a big Party event, all the churches were invited and somebody would bless the table. The Young Pioneers would have considered that there was a very healthy relationship between Church and state and would have been part of any discussions around developmental issues. That view notwithstanding, priests were always conscious of being watched. Justice and peace matters were particularly sensitive. So, whether they were saying mass or talking with a group of lay leaders, priests had to be aware that there was someone there among them listening and reporting back to the Party. It was not unusual for priests to find themselves chastised by the Party and told that whatever they had said was not acceptable to the Party, and to be more careful in the future.

When John moved from Nkhamenya after almost three years, to the northern cathedral parish of St. Peter's, in Mzuzu, it was to quite a different type of parish. It was mainly urban, but reached out into a small rural area as well. The urban part of the parish had a very strong Catholic community of 10-15,000 people. The idea of the basic Christian community continued to flourish here also. There was not the same sense of alienation in urban centres in Malawi as had developed in other African cities because of the Banda government's emphasis on agricultural development. Besides, contact with the home area and the extended family remained strong. There was constant movement of people to the urban areas and back to the homelands. People pursuing education stayed with relatives in the town. At holiday time, and for special occasions likes marriages or funerals, people always went from the cities and towns back to their homes of origin.

In Mzuzu, the small Christian communities had the extra challenge of having people from a number of ethnic groups, because people had come from all over the country to work in the city. There were tensions from time to time, not the least of which was the language. As shown earlier, for historical reasons connected with colonisation, the best education in the country was to be had in the northern region. Because of that many northerners worked in teaching and the civil and government services; they were looked upon with jealousy and suspicion by many others in the central and southern region. If there was to be any questioning of the government, it was likely to come from the northern region. Levi Mumba, who led the North Nyasaland Native Association, organised the Native Civil Servants Association, which could be considered the first ever trade union in Malawi, was a Tongan from the northern region. At one time the language of the north, Chitumbuka, was actually banned from the national radio.

People in the parish from the central or southern region wanted matters to be discussed in English or Chichewa, but the locals wanted Chitumbuka to be used. Despite such difficulties, the communities tried to transcend the cultural and ethnic differences to work together. For the most part, they were successful in that, and concentrated on building up and consolidating the Christian community.

They were able to deal with matters concerning health, education and development. The more difficult issues were around poverty, unemployment and justice. With the more mobile urban population of a city, it was difficult to know whom to trust when speaking out. There would have been Catholics in the police, the army and the civil service. There would have been very committed members of the Malawi Congress Party in the groups also. So the issues were never faced head-on. Issues of justice and peace were incorporated in catechesis in a very tentative manner and those preparing for baptism into the community were exposed to them, albeit in a very gentle way.

In Mzuzu the same atmosphere of fear and oppression prevailed. On one occasion, a migrant worker returned from the mines in South Africa flush with cash and treated his friends to a crate of beer in the local bar. Grateful for his generosity, one of the friends lifted his glass and wished long life to his benefactor. He was tapped on the shoulder and reminded that nobody in the country was allowed to wish 'long life' to anybody other than the president, and the unfortunate well-wisher was taken away. Nobody could be named president of an organisation because the only president in the country could be H. Kamuzu Banda. The presiding member of any group could, at most, be chairman. This notion of absolute superiority of the leader was carried through to the point of absurdity in the ruling on the hanging of Banda's portraits in private homes and public places. His pictures had to be higher than any other picture on the walls and had to be positioned so that it was the first picture seen when entering the building. There were plenty of Malawi Young Pioneers and Youth Leaguers patrolling to ensure that these rulings were enforced under threat of detention.

One of the parishioners of St. Peter's, Mr. M-, was denounced to the authorities by his sister for a remark he had made. In a dispute over a plot of land, in a moment of anger, he told his sister that the only thing she was good for was dancing for Kamuzu. She reported him to the local Party officials and he was detained within the hour. On hearing of the detention, John went to the police station and asked to see Mr. M-. The police, not used to being challenged in this way, made it very clear that Fr. John Roche should go back to his parish and not meddle in matters that did not concern him. However, he persisted and eventually they allowed him to see Mr. M-. His cell was tiny, with no washing facilities. The toilet was a bucket in one corner. Normally a fastidious man, Mr. M—had not been allowed to wash in two days. John went away and got some food and clean clothes. He was allowed give these to the prisoner, but there was a growing sense of personal threat with this and subsequent visits. John continued to visit, asking each time when Mr M—'s trial would be. After a month of this persistent questioning, the officer in charge of the prison phoned John to tell him that his presence was unacceptable and that if he persisted, something could happen to him. Eventually Mr. M—was transferred elsewhere without notice. Despite many attempts to locate him, he could not be found. When he was released two years later at the age of sixty-one, he was a broken man, physically and emotionally, who would not, or could not, talk about his prison experiences.

Another parishioner was detained for non-payment of taxes. As the taxes were arbitrary, one never knew what exactly the liability was, so detention was always a risk. Again, efforts to find where the man was detained were in vain. He was released after two months' detention, during which he was sexually abused.

The sense of frustration with the living conditions of the ordinary people continued to grow in John. Though on very good terms with his bishop, from time to time John found himself in conflict with him over Party attitudes. This was difficult for both men because apart from being accustomed to living under Banda from the early days, Bishop Jean-Louis Jobidon was in poor health. He was not in any physical condition to challenge the authorities. Jobidon was a kindly man, with a gentle and caring attitude for his priests. He continually struggled with problems of Church/Party relations. John understood this and felt compassion for the man on a personal level. The most senior bishop, Archbishop Chiona, was a Malawian national, and it is likely that Bishop Jobidon felt any initiative in challenging the government should come from Chiona as leader and as an indigenous bishop.

The only forum open to John to attempt some criticism of the status quo in the light of the gospels was in his preaching. Doing this was no less risky than making the comments in a more secular environment. Mzuzu was a large city and had a significant police and government civil service population. He was told more than once that his preaching was straying into forbidden territory. But there was some small satisfaction in responding to the oppression both as an individual and as Church.

There was also the difficulty of the Christians bringing a divided message. Coming fresh from a post-Vatican II training, ecumenism was a new and shinning ideal. In Malawi, however, ecumenism was not a priority for any of the churches. Still full of enthusiasm for the ecumenical ideal, when John first arrived in Nkhamenya as a young priest, he called on the other Christian churches and groups in to introduce himself, and was received kindly by everyone. Up to 1980 there were significant numbers of expatriates in leadership positions in the Presbyterian Church and they would not interact with the Catholic mission or dialogue in any way and there was much latent hostility. The Malawian Presbyterians on the other hand interacted more positively although in a limited way.

Many months after John's arrival, the Presbyterians, who were the most significant Christian group in the country generally, and numerically the biggest church in the north, were having a gathering of their elders, and their leader, a Malawian, invited representatives from all the other Christian churches to attend. They participated in a prayer and afterwards they were invited for light refreshments. While enjoying a cup of tea, a small group of expatriates came in. One of the group, a woman whose accent announced that she was from Northern Ireland, went around shaking hands, smiling and greeting everybody. In his grey and black clerical outfit, John might have been another 'reverend' and was assumed to be so. When their host made the formal introductions, the lady froze when she heard John was a Catholic priest and ignored him for the rest of the visit. When it was time to leave, she did not participate in the formalities of the goodbyes. When driving home, the catechist, a Malawian person who had accompanied John asked what had been said to the woman. Curious to know what prompted the question, John inquired a little more, to which the catechist replied that whatever John had said, it must have been something terrible. He described the look of 'anger and hate' on woman's face. When John further explained that she was actually a compatriot, the catechist shook his head and said that sometimes it was very difficult to understand white people.

The negative feelings associated with not proclaiming the gospel as it was meant, were compounded by the scandal of the divided Christian message that at times was more about territorial influence than the message of love and reconciliation. Ecumenism was a dessicated and lifeless concept in Malawi until the latter part of the 1980s

Having spent three years in St. Peter's parish, Mzuzu, John was then sent to teach in St. Patrick's minor seminary in Rumphi. While it would not have been his first choice, because of his pastoral leanings, he had increased administrative responsibility that was to prove useful in his next appointment. The activities of the Party even had an impact on John's arrival in Rumphi. Pope John Paul II was scheduled to visit Ireland in October 1979, but John had to return to Malawi for the opening of term, and therefore would miss the historic visit. When he arrived in Rumphi, his disappointment at missing the papal visit was compounded by the fact that the start of term had been postponed. The Party had decided to hold a regional meeting there and the seminary could not re-open for two weeks. If he had known this, John could have remained in Ireland for the first-ever visit of a pope to his home country.

The atmosphere of fear and watchfulness was as much part of the seminary life as it was of every other aspect of life in Malawi. It was certain that some seminarians were reporting back to the Party on all that was discussed in tuition. This led to a certain curtailment of discussion. However, shortly into the appointment at Rumphi, a new opportunity was offered to John by the Society.

In 1978 St. Patrick's Missionary Society decided at their general chapter, in Ireland, that there with forty men working in the region, there were sufficient numbers to warrant the creation of a new region, which they called Central Africa. It would have a regional superior with responsibility for Zambia and Malawi. John was elected the first regional superior by his peers. This meant a complete change of focus and location. The regional house was situated in Lilongwe, the capital, which was in the central region.

— Chapter 8 —
Regional superior

As regional superior, John Roche's role changed completely. Aged thirty-two, he was now responsible for the welfare of the forty men in the Society's mission in Zambia and Malawi, and was no longer as deeply involved in parish work. Ordinarily, the job of the regional superior was to sort out problems, arrange flights home, deal with emergencies and generally act as a sort of 'pater familias' within the Society. As well as being a 'fixer' of practical problems, the regional was also involved in the all-important ongoing formation of the priests, being spiritually and emotionally supportive of them in their mission.

Sometimes this moral support of the priests had its worrying aspect. In March 1976, Fr. Pádraig Ó Máille, a member of St. Patrick' Missionary Society, was offered a post lecturing in the English department of Chancellor College, University of Malawi. In August, 1976 he came face to face with the reality of detentions. A neighbour and colleague was detained. Soon afterwards another colleague was detained. No reason was given for the detentions. Through this experience and friendships formed within the college, Fr. Ó Máille, who prior to this had reached the accommodation all the missionary priests had with the state machinery, had now become conscientised to the great injustice that was political detention. Many senior academic staff of the College had been detained, without trial, by the authorities. The blanket accusation was 'subversion.' Fr. Ó Máille became active with others in secretly supplying reading and writing materials to detainees and channelling news to them through the help of a sympathetic prison guard. Through his lectures and involvement with the Writers' Workshop in the College, he debated the political state of the country with the students, albeit in metaphor using poetry as the vehicle. It would be standard operating procedure of the authorities to have people 'planted' in the College to report back to them. The 'plant' could be anybody – a cleaner, a secretary, a student or a lecturer.

While admiring and being challenged by the courage and activism of Pádraig Ó Máille, John Roche, as regional, at times had concerns for Ó Máille's safety. While offering his moral support, all he could urge was care and discretion. Expatriates were not usually treated with the same barbarism by the government as the Malawian people. For them breaking the rules usually meant expulsion at very short notice. But one could never be sure what might happen and car 'accidents' always remained a possibility. Once or twice, at particularly sensitive times, John went to stay a night with his confrère, just to be another presence in the house at night, in case there would be a visit by the police.

While not active in particular situations to bring about justice for individual people, through the forum of AMRIM and ARIMA (the representative groups of male and female religious in Malawi), John had some confidence that change was possible at an institutional level. This would in turn, he believed, make a difference to the people as a whole and perhaps bring about the fundamental change that would be necessary to create a more open and just society. The think-tank of the AMRIM/ARIMA forum notwithstanding, the fact that Ó Máille was doing what John felt he ought to be doing was a constant challenge and in ways, an uncomfortable commentary on the gap between his faith and his actions.

In discussions with the priests on the type of function the regional superior should have within Malawi, it was decided that the job should not become completely divorced from contact with the people. Therefore, it was decided that the regional would also act as curate to the small contiguous parish of St. Kizito. The regional would have no developmental role within the parish, but would still maintain contact with the people albeit to a limited extent. The importance of not withdrawing from the reality of people's lives into comfortable administration was vividly displayed one Sunday morning. St. Kizito's parish had a outstation in Mtsiriza, one of the many shantytowns surrounding Lilongwe. Life was very tough for the people here, there was great poverty and basic facilities were virtually non-existent. The missionaries, who included Fr. Michael Power SPS, had worked with the people to bring water to the area, contributing in some way to the alleviation of some of the worst effects of poverty.

John arrived early at the church for mass and was surprised to see nobody around. People would usually start congregating as early as a half an hour before mass time. But there was nobody in sight. Then a group of people came into view heading down through the village. A circle began forming and there were a number of young people watching. Getting out of his car, John went over to find out what was happening. A woman, a parishioner of St. Kizito's, was bent over trying to protect herself. She was covered in mud and dirt and a Young Pioneer, a big, sturdy man, was beating her with a stick. He yelled at her, "Dance! Faster! Faster! John asked the Young Pioneer why he was beating the woman. "None of your business" was the abrupt reply. John persisted saying it was his business as the woman was a parishioner. He was told that the woman had sneered at Kamuzu and now must be taught a lesson, whereupon, the Young Pioneer turned on her and struck a vicious blow. John attempted to intervene again, and was told very clearly that if he asked any more questions, he would face the consequences. He stood back and watched as the woman was made run around the area being beaten as she ran. This was a usual tactic of the Young Pioneers, and done to set an example and terrorise others into submission.

When the punishment group was gone, people began to appear and come to the church. Very angry, John asked them if nothing could be done. Helpless themselves, and knowing it could be their turn next time, all the people could suggest was that John go to the bishop. He did this the following day. The bishop asked for evidence of the attack. John explained there were a number of young people who witnessed it. He was told their evidence would not be sufficient. And that was that. The protest was dismissed. There was nothing to be done. The anger grew, but rooted in that anger was a sense of shame that he had backed down before the Young Pioneer. While the anger was slowly growing, the shame was also growing. Yet again, John had witnessed a grave injustice, and yet again he stood by and watched. In retrospect his attempted intervention seemed a feeble effort. Perhaps the woman had received a few less blows, but that could be no consolation or ease to conscience. The gap between faith and action was now becoming a running sore.

While there was no public discussion on the state of repression in the country and its challenge to the Christian message, the leaders of the various religious groups came together for discussions. Within Malawi there was the male religious organisation AMRIM (Association of Male Religious in Malawi), and the female religious organisation, ARIMA (Association of Religious in Malawi). Within Zambia also there were associations of religious groups meeting with each other. The groups in both countries met once a year. It was an opportunity for the exchange of ideas and concerns. The Zambian group had much more freedom within Zambia to criticise the state of governance.

AMRIM and ARIMA met separately twice a year. The discussions within these groups were then brought back to the individual orders, so that the level of awareness among the religious was increasing all the time. The combined group brought out a challenging document on justice and evangelisation. It represented an important step forward for them as a declaration of where they stood on matters of justice. There was a great sense of solidarity and a sense of finally doing something positive in face of the state repression. Having written the document, a decision was taken by the group to lobby the bishops. The groups felt that it could energise the bishops and give them courage to know that they had the solid backing of all the religious institutions. There was a great sense of hope and a sense that perhaps this might be the beginning of a new journey - one that might lead to worthwhile change.

The document was clear and unequivocal as it examined the Church's role within Malawi. It praised that which was praiseworthy, including the contribution of the Church to health, education and development. It noted the efforts to increase participation of the lay people in the pastoral life of the Church, including a very positive role for women. It also mentioned the increase in vocations to the priesthood and religious life. It noted that *'inner conversion within the Church is leading to less antagonistic and competitive relations with the other churches.'* Having demonstrated what was good about the Church in Malawi, there was no complacency evident in the AMRIM/ARIMA document. It did not shy away from that which was less praiseworthy and detailed those as carefully as the positive aspects. It mentioned that in some dioceses the relationship between the expatriates and the local church personnel was not all it should be. That the lifestyle of some of the clergy and religious often appeared *'too rich and too comfortable when seen in the context of the people amongst whom we work.'* It is also stark in its admission that *'some clergy and religious lead a double life, disrupting families and giving counter-witness'* to the gospel.

The document went on to examine the socio-political field and clearly laid out the areas of concern: the lack of freedom of expression of the people; concerns about the teaching of religion in schools; the emerging pattern of more and more wealth being controlled by a smaller and smaller elite. The document also talked about the breakdown in society due to increasing abuse of alcohol and the growth of organised prostitution.

Having detailed what was negative about the Church and society, the document went on to list the actions the Church could take to improve the situation. Of the sixteen 'suggested lines of action' no less that six referred to improvements the Church could make in its own approach to the practise of faith, and these were listed first. The document went on to suggest that other improvements could only be made with the support of the bishops and listed these.

The AMRIM/ARIMA document was probably the most serious attempt to institute change within Malawi since independence. It was a concise, well-considered appraisal of Church and state and offered well-thought out ways how conditions might be improved for everybody. It was presented to the Malawi Episcopal Conference in this spirit on 25th March, 1983 concluding with "*we present these considerations to the Episcopal Conference without whose support and guidance the Church in Malawi shall never be able to achieve a concerted effort and unity in its work for justice.*"

The lobbying of the bishops achieved nothing. The document was assessed, point by point, by a sub-committee of the episcopal conference at a meeting on 22nd April, 1983. Rather than using it as a starting-point for dialogue on how the Church might move forward, the document was appraised in terms of its criticisms. Where there were criticisms of the Church, the long-winded response of the bishops was defensive and equivocal: "*it was noted.. that before you start analysing a position of your superiors one should at all times first seek to meet the person in private and share with him the common problems.*" And, "*It is only fair that the religious remain fair in their dealing with the people, but they should not create confusion among God's people. It should be mentioned and made known that it's only the bishops who can make statements on given issues as they think appropriate at the opportune time. The committee* [Espiscopal sub-committee] *made it known that* **Jesus Christ worked towards compromise on issues or on established structures which were opposed to God's law.**" [Author's emphasis]. In the assessment of the socio-political comments, the bishops had this to say: "*It should be borne in mind that politics is never primarily the field of the Church. It is only through proper religious instructions and proper preaching of the Gospel that the Church is able to form and quieten the conscience of the people.*" What was meant by 'quieten the conscience of the people' is not clear from the document.

At a subsequent meeting between representatives of AMRIM/ARIMA and the episcopal conference, the bishops thanked the leaders for the work they did on the preparation of the document, but that was the end of the dialogue. There was no change in attitude. The bishops carried on as meekly and acquiescent as before. There was a real sense of frustration among the religious groups. They felt that having worked so hard on producing a discussion document that would bring the issues of justice into an open forum and having the initiative shelved immediately showed a complete lack of respect for them as a group, and indicated a lack of confidence in them by their leaders. The bishops also demonstrated a lack of confidence in their own function as leaders. There had been a real hope that if the bishops knew the support that existed for them, they might create some initiative that would allow public discussion to take place.

While the population at large was terrorised into mute submission, the Catholic students at the University of Malawi were not so docile. They knew that an international organisation such as the Church had power to speak out, quite apart from it being the duty of the Church to speak out against the oppression of the Malawian people by their government. In 1983, Fr. Pádraig Ó Máille in his capacity as chaplain to the Catholic students of Chancellor College had to report to the Malawi episcopal conference. He consulted with the students to see what issues they wanted addressed by the bishops and the Church. Some days later, they presented him with a letter:

> *"We, the Catholic students of Chancellor College, would like our bishops to speak out on matters of justice and peace. We realise that this may involve the church in suffering, but this is the challenge of the Gospel. We believe that if our Bishops gave a lead, our ordinary Christians would support them. We are always very proud when we read in the papers or hear on the radio how the bishops in neighbouring countries condemn the injustices and exploitation by their governments against ordinary people. We do not want our bishops to be like our politicians"*[1]

But just as with the AMRIM/ARIMA document on justice, the students' plea for leadership and identification with the gospel message met with little success.

The most likely person in authority within the Catholic Church to give focus to the yearning for justice was the controversial Bishop Kalilombe of Lilongwe who was out of the country at the time of the AMRIM/ARIMA document. A Malawian, he was a member of the White Fathers and was a shrewd and intelligent man. He was a brilliant and charismatic preacher, and in some ways, intellectually was the heart of the episcopal conference. He was a very strong advocate of the small Christian communities and was very committed to and in touch with the people and the realities of their lives. Once on a visit to a neighbouring parish when John Roche was in Nkhamenya in the mid 1970s, the bishop's car was physically lifted up by the parishioners for about the last half-mile or so. In a country where the public honour and praise can only be conferred on one man, the President, this was wont to bring undesirable attention on Bishop Kalilombe.

Reaction from government to the bishop's work, preaching and increasing popularity was swift and decisive. The bishop was expelled. At the time of his expulsion there was a lot of rumour about his personal life, and not without foundation. There were suggestions of inappropriate behaviour and sexual liaisons with certain women. Popular though he was, people were concerned that the Church should take whatever action was necessary if he

---

[1] Ó Máille, Pádraig, *Living Dangerously: a memoir of political change in Malawi.*
(Dudu Nsomba Publications, Glasgow,1999. p 42)

was involved in conduct unbecoming a bishop. Either he should be reprimanded appropriately or given an opportunity to change his behaviour. Before the Church could investigate the matter fully and arrive at the truth, the Party intervened. The President said that he had heard of the bishop's immorality, that the people were being disturbed by it and it was only right that he was sent out of the country.

While there was acceptance of the fact that the bishop most likely had a case to answer, nevertheless, many believed that it was not his suspected immorality that had him expelled, rather it was his immense popularity. That fact that he was also from the central region, Banda's own territory, further added to his undesirability from the Party point of view.

That Malawi should lose such a charismatic person in a position of leadership brought into focus yet again, the negative impact of the imposition of celibacy on a particular culture. Celibacy is not always an issue of sex for many African cultures, Malawi included. In certain ethnic groups, the holy person will, at some stage in their lives, lead a celibate life by choice. They would feel that they were called to this as part of their ministry. For others, celibacy is an unnatural imposition of the ideas and rules of another culture.

In Malawi, common to the various ethnic groups, there is a very strong sense of connection. A person is connected to his/her ancestors, connected to nature, connected to the living relatives of the immediate family, the extended family, the community and connected to the unborn. Especially in patrilineal societies, the ability to procreate is highly regarded. It is about continuing the name of the family, of the clan and of the community. If a man is infertile, it is a major shame. Apart from his individual shame, he is also shamed insofar as he has failed in his wider duty to the community. Within the Malawian cultures and many other African cultures, a person has identity through the connectedness of things – 'I am because of all of those who came before me; I will be because of those who come after me and will remember me. If I am at fault in breaking the connection between the ancestors and those yet to be born, I have failed in my whole reason for living.' In John Roche's pastoral experience, infertility was a major problem and very likely to result in suicide. Given the power of connectedness with the African culture, celibacy in the African context can be counter-cultural. It has nothing to do with restraint or with sacrifice, it is, for many, an alien concept. It was no less significant for the women in society. It was very important to them to be able to bear children, to be 'fruitful', to be the bearers of the next generation of their families, and by extension the whole community.

Even in John's time in Mzuzu, there were those who fully believed that the nuns in the hospital across the way were really the priests' wives, that there was a tunnel linking the residences! They had difficulty believing that priests and nuns had made lifetime commitments to a celibate way of life. The people would have had great respect for the sacred and those involved with the sacred, whether of their own religion or not. While a strongly patriarchal country, in both the patrilineal and matrilineal societies, where men would have difficulty taking orders from women, those working with the religious sisters who ran the hospitals had tremendous respect for and appreciation of those who have given their lives to come and work in Malawi. Given the cultural attitudes and the great respect for the sacred among the Malawian people, they were likely to have been ashamed of Bishop Kalilombe's behaviour, but he might have been the prophetic voice they so desperately needed.

Through the 1980s the anger and frustration with the political situation, with the leaders who were not giving leadership and with the knowledge that he was not an obvious counter-sign in the oppressive culture, continued to nag at John's conscience. There was the constant dilemma of whether to speak up and be expelled within twenty-four hours or to keep his head down and continue to work for the people. Discussions with other people, both Malawian and expatriates, suggested that it was better to accept the situation, no matter how difficult, and continue to minister to the people in whatever ways were possible. When the new elections for the regional superior came up in 1984, John was re-elected as regional and happy to continue in the post. He found he had an ability to do the job, he liked it and living in Lilongwe, the capital, had certain advantages. Because of the all-pervasive atmosphere of fear and distrust, real friendships of depth were very difficult to form with the Malawian people. They were terrorised into almost total silence. Yet some lasting friendships with Malawians were possible and have been maintained. In Lilongwe, there were a number of expatriates working in various institutions. Though the transient nature of the expatriate population meant the friendships were more superficial, at times it was a relief to be able to relax and chat where every word was not weighed for meaning and how it might be interpreted.

To the background of great disappointment with the leadership of the Church, John, throughout his time as regional, made the decision to remain silent and continue working. It was a decision not easily made and it cost much in terms of conscience and the promise to witness to the gospel message, to bring good news to the poor and tell the captives that they were free. But change was in the air, in a way that John could never have considered or have chosen.

— Chapter 9 —

Apostolic Administrator

A s regional superior, it was part of John's remit to communicate Society policy to those priests working in the field. Each year a meeting of regional superiors was held in Ireland, to which men from East, West and Central Africa, the Caribbean and South America came. It was a time to discuss mission policy in general, to learn how other leaders were dealing with certain problems and difficulties, and to maintain a sense of unity and cohesion within the Society as a whole.

As these meetings were mainly concerned with administration of the Society, the areas of justice and peace and their priority within the Society were discussed on the broader canvas of Society policy. Particular problems within specific countries were not really discussed in detail. However, listening to the Brazilian experience and learning of the courage of Helder Càmara, John could only wish for the same kind of leadership within Malawi – for some charismatic, courageous figure within the Church to give voice to the oppressed people and their suffering.

In 1987, when in Ireland for the regionals' meeting, John took a few weeks' holidays to spend some time with his mother and extended family in Athlone. While there, a telephone call from the Society's superior general shook John to the very core of his being. Picking up the receiver, he heard the familiar voice of Fr. Peter Finegan greeting him and going on immediately to say that John had been summoned to Rome and was expected to go at once. On asking the reason for such a summons, he was told that the matter was *sub secreto* and could not be discussed. Fr. Finegan would not be drawn any further on the matter, save to say that he would phone again in the morning and would need a reply.

A peremptory summons to Rome could not mean good news. John's first thought was: what had he done? He tried to recall any situation in which he had been involved that might have given offence. Nothing came to mind, but that was cold comfort. The fact that a priest could be 'delated' to Rome anonymously by a disgruntled or vindictive person often resulted in an inversion of the normal judicial process where a person was innocent until proven guilty, which meant that anything was possible. Having spent a distressed and sleepless night, John came to a decision by morning. Telephoning Fr. Finegan, he told him that he was not going to Rome voluntarily without some idea of what lay in wait for him. He was then told that the matter concerned Mzuzu diocese and the superior general would say no more.

Before John had left Malawi for Ireland, some of the Society's priests in Mzuzu diocese had approached him, telling him that his name was being mentioned in connection with some senior administrative post within the church, possibly that of bishop to replace Bishop Jobidon who was in poor health. They were concerned about this, as the indigenous priests, members of ADCOM (Association for Diocesan Clergy of Malawi) were anxious that any new appointment of a bishop should be a local man. The priests would deeply resent any imposition of another expatriate. Within the episcopal conference, there were still two expatriate bishops: Bishop Jobidon of Mzuzu and Bishop Assolari of Mangochi. As a strong advocate of local leadership, John Roche would have found himself in agreement with the ADCOM members, and voiced this opinion openly and so dismissed the rumours as pure speculation. Now, perhaps it was not just speculation after all.

Setting out for Rome in August, John considered what might lie ahead of him. He had concluded that Bishop Jobidon, who had been his bishop and whom he knew well and liked, was going to retire on health grounds and that a replacement was needed. While Jobidon might have had difficulty confronting the difficult issues within Malawi, he was at heart a good man who had given the better part of his life to the cause of the Church. He was good to his priests and cared for them in a fatherly manner. He was suffering from a serious heart condition and needed to retire from what was an extremely stressful job in a very stressful environment. Wondering what he might be asked to do, John considered his position. He was quite happy as regional in Lilongwe. He still had another two years to serve and did not see any reason why this should change. He marshalled his thoughts and prepared his case.

On arrival in Rome he met with the Society's representative there. Together they went to the offices of the Congregation for the Propagation of the Faith. There, they met with two monsignors who wasted no time telling John that Bishop Jobidon was to retire soon and that John was chosen to be the apostolic administrator (acting bishop). Having had time to think on the outward journey, John laid out his arguments. One, there were a number of very good Malawian priests who would be suited to the job; two, the local clergy would not readily accept the imposition of yet another expatriate; three, John had been out of Mzuzu for almost seven years, apart from twice-yearly visits, and therefore out of touch with the diocese. He set out every objection he could think of and the monsignors listened politely, dismissed the objections out of hand and re-stated the original request that John accept the post. Unwilling to be forced into acceptance, John asked for more time to consider the proposal. This was willingly granted with the suggestion that he return by 4.00pm with his answer! The mien of the monsignors left no doubt of what they expected that answer to be.

John spent the next few hours alone to consider what was being asked of him. He tried to pray for discernment. He considered all he knew to be true about the difficulties in accepting such a post, yet there was that tiny core of certainty deep within him saying that this was the way he was meant to go. In ways, the offer of apostolic administrator seemed so unbelievable, that he thought that maybe there was a reason for this, a reason that he had yet to understand. He remembered the motto he had chosen for his ordination card: 'Thy will be done.' The submission of the will of Jesus to the Father no matter what the cost was something that impinged on John's faith and mission. While he wished that this cup might pass him by, he knew that he could give only one answer when he returned to Propaganda Fide.

In accepting the appointment of apostolic administrator, John made it clear that he would accept it for a period of three years only; it was not to lead to his appointment as bishop and he would prepare a local priest for the position of Bishop of Mzuzu. And he wanted the agreement in writing! Considering his great anxiety when he first received the summons to Rome, John found no small amusement in the fact that he was now laying down the conditions of his appointment. The monsignors then brought him to meet a cardinal who gave him a crozier and a ring. Looking at the accoutrements of office, John asked why he needed them, he was not a bishop after all, he was just an administrator. The cardinal told him that he would need them for confirmations, official functions and suchlike. They were the signs of his authority. On inquiring the nature of his 'authority', he was told, a little sardonically, that he was 'like a little pope in your own diocese!' He was also told that he had been bestowed with the title 'Monsignor'. The letters of appointment, in Latin, were read and handed over. Monsignor John Roche had become the acting Bishop of Mzuzu.

Oddly enough, the sight of the ring and crozier gave the appointment a reality that was almost disturbing. The trappings of 'authority' did not sit well with the idea of something that was only an interim measure. While he used the crozier because of its pastoral symbolism, the ring he put away and never used.

There was no public announcement made about the appointment, so that the Society would have adequate time to make the administrative changes that were necessary for a quiet, smooth hand-over of the regional's job in

Lilongwe. The matter was kept confidential between the Vatican, Kiltegan and John Roche. It was decided that the announcement would be held until John was on the aeroplane and heading to Mzuzu in early November 1987. In the air, flying to Mzuzu from Lilongwe, the inevitability of what he was about to face reduced John to tears. He had left a satisfying life behind him in Lilongwe. He could only guess at what lay ahead of him.

There was a small welcoming party at the airport. In general, the laity and the religious were quite happy at his appointment. The male clergy, however, were furious. Even during John's time in Mzuzu as a curate, he was aware that the clergy there wanted Bishop Jobidon to retire. The priests made no secret of the fact that they were ready to take over the administration of the diocese. A petition had even been sent to Rome about it. John would have been quite sympathetic to their cause and while saying that the time was not yet here, he encouraged them to be patient, that their time would come. Now here he was, imposed on them by Rome, the embodiment of all they resented in the white authority telling them what was good for them. It was no help that John was a young man, just forty years of age. As the Malawian priests saw it, it was possible that he could be left in position for another thirty years or so. No matter how many times John tried to tell them that he was an interim appointment for a short period, they dismissed his arguments as nothing more than the usual white man's rhetoric telling the black man in his own country that he knew better than they did what was best for them.

Some of the priests actually told John to his face that they did not want him and hoped that he would get out quickly. Others were not quite so aggressive, but were quite hurt, that knowing their feelings so well, John should accept the appointment, and they made this quite clear to him. During his time as regional, John had visited the diocese about twice a year. He could see that Bishop Jobidon was becoming more and more ill and consequently unable to give leadership in the diocese. Jobidon had wanted to retire for quite some time, but had to wait until the authorities in the Vatican allowed him. The priests of Mzuzu were becoming more unsettled and were telling John that they needed leadership. Sympathetic though he would have been towards Bishop Jobidon, knowing how ill the man was and the implications of that for the diocese, he agreed with them. Now suddenly he was their leader, deeply resented and unwanted. There was a small number of older priests, one or two of whom would have believed that they ought to have been appointed. They were quite influential within the association of priests. It only needed one or two strong personalities to sway the opinion of the group, with the result that John faced very strong and overt hostility.

While he had no sense of fear about his personal safety, he was concerned about acceptance as administrator. If he was not accepted, he could not lead. If he could not lead, there would be no real progress in the diocese. If there was no progress in the diocese, the resentment of the priests would only increase and so the circle would continue. His situation was not made any easier by a difficult decision that had to be made within a few months of arriving in the diocese when he felt it necessary to reject a candidate for the priesthood in the face of strong opposition from his college of consultors.

Amid the criticism and the disquiet all John could do was hold onto the conviction that he had to do what he believed was right, no matter how unpopular it would make him. In this he felt a strong connection to his father, who had died when John was about nineteen years of age. Jack Roche had a profound respect for truth and integrity. He continually tried to instil this love of truth and the courage to face it in his children. When John found himself alone and isolated by the priests in Mzuzu, he took comfort from the fact that he was being true to what he believed to be right. To some, leadership appeared to settle easy on his shoulders, but within it was a constant struggle between what he wanted to do and what he had to do.

It was only now that the lessons of leadership learned in the job as regional superior came into their own. They enabled him to deal with a very difficult, lonely situation and confirmed his conviction that as much as he did not want this particular job, he would give it the very best of which he was capable and hope that that would be good enough.

* * * * *

All told, the worst of the resentment lasted about nine months. However, his attendance at the first episcopal conference meeting in February changed John's own attitude considerably. Given what appeared to be the complete lack of response by the bishops to the major human rights abuses, John could hardly believe his ears when he heard the level of discussion at the meeting. All issues were being discussed with great sincerity and commitment. Listening to what was said at the meeting, John remembered the many times he preached about taking risks and being a counter-cultural figure in society. His own words as a preacher now began to challenge him.

At the meeting he did not bring up the issue of the attitude of the priests in the diocese to him. While he felt that the bishops were likely to be aware of what was going on, he did not want to appear to blame and criticise his priests. If the bishops had raised the subject, he would have discussed it. Since they did not, he let the matter rest. Coming out of the meeting, he realised that he had a choice – to continue fearfully through the next three years, tolerating and accommodating the resentment directed at him, or he could take the initiative and lead as he ought.

One of the first things he did was to organise a mini-synod in the diocese. It encompassed the views and energies of the laity, priests and religious. A five-year plan was drawn up for the development of the church and its outreach in the diocese. Given the fact that John was willing to gather the people and listen to them and incorporate their vision, the attitudes of those around him began to mellow. They began to realise that he was not there to impose his ideas upon them; rather his function was to listen and help direct the way forward. As the people began to have input in and could claim ownership of the development of their church, relationships continued to improve. Right through the rest of 1988 and into 1989 John immersed himself in the pastoral work of the diocese, making himself available as much as possible to the people for renewal programmes, adult formation programmes, confirmations and so forth. He also instituted annual programmes for the on-going formation of the clergy, and these were well accepted by the priests.

As a leader, John saw as part of his function the need to conscientise those priests and religious working with the people, and he encouraged discussion on the matter. Preaching in his sermons he sought to conscientise the people at large, encouraging them to discern between what was acceptable in their treatment by government and what was not acceptable. Whenever he addressed gatherings of church leaders and youth leaders, he constantly reflected justice and peace issues through the gospel message. There were times when he had to confront the authorities publicly. On one occasion, a member of the local clergy was accused of respecting neither the national language (Chichewa) nor a particular ethnic group in the area, and was detained. When John returned to the town and heard of the detention, he went straight to the police station. He demanded to see the most senior officer and refused to deal with anyone else. He remained in the police station, refusing to leave until he was given details of the accusations. He argued that as the priest was in his care, he was entitled to this information. Eventually, after eight hours or more, the police, unused to being confronted in this way, released the man without charge.

Something similar happened with workers in the compound of the bishop's house. A number of workers were accused of some misdemeanour by the Young Pioneers, who proceeded to confiscate goods belonging to them from their houses within the compound. No warrant was produced. John called the Young Pioneers to his office and told them that they had no right to enter the compound and if there was a problem, they must come with the correct paperwork and discuss the matter with him. Again, unused to being challenged, the Young Pioneers left.

Within the episcopal conference he gained confidence when he realised that although the bishops would have preferred a Malawian, they accepted John's presence. Though an expatriate and the youngest member there, he was given the same opportunities to speak as anyone else. In retrospect, John realised that the bishops may have found him difficult to deal with at first. He would have been robust in his discussions and urging action in issues around justice, peace and good governance. Having been pleasantly surprised that all issues were discussed at this level, there was a certain frustration that all the talk did not lead to some action. There was also a sense of being part of a broader Church when the conference was asked, through the pro-nuncio, to contribute documents to various Synods being held in Rome.

In early 1989, the bishops of Malawi learned that their invitation to Pope John Paul II to visit the country had been accepted. When they heard that the pope had plans to visit Central Africa they issued their invitation through the pro-nuncio, Archbishop Barbaro, who was based in Lusaka, Zambia. When the acceptance came, there was only about eight to ten weeks to prepare for the visit. The pro-nuncio, realising John's administrative and organisational skills, suggested that he might head up the planning. Knowing at once what an insult it would be to the bishops to have not only the youngest, but an expatriate, to take charge of the organisation, John declined. While he realised from his experience that action was not the strongest suit of the bishops, it was still better that a Malawian be seen to be in charge. This was to change, however, when with about three weeks to go to the papal visit, the pro-nuncio met with the conference and discovered that plans were way behind schedule. He immediately insisted that John become the national organiser for the event. This in no way endeared John to the man who had been in charge. In order to make things work as smoothly as possible, John continued with the planning, but suggested that the man who had been in charge should remain as the public face of the conference organisation.

The government was quite well disposed towards the visit. It was an opportunity for some positive world publicity for the country. The publicity gained from the revelations of Amnesty International about the appalling prison conditions could be counteracted in some way by the visit of a world leader. The government put finance and manpower at the disposal of the organisers. Without this input, the visit could not have happened. However, the contribution of the government brought a whole new set of problems. The visit of the pope was a pastoral visit to his flock in Malawi. It was not a political visit of a head of state. The pope had been invited to Malawi by the bishops, albeit with the government's approval, and the bishops were anxious that the visit would not be hijacked for political ends.

The single biggest problem was the place of His Excellency, the Life President, H.K. Banda. This was a man who had great difficulty accepting that praise and admiration could be given to anyone other than himself. The Party functionaries wanted to dictate the terms of Banda's publicity during the visit. They wanted Banda's poster to appear alongside those of the pope. It was agreed that Banda's poster could appear at the airport, because that was to be the official government welcome. After that, it was a purely pastoral visit, therefore there was to be no government intervention. John continued to resist all attempts to deflect attention to Banda.

The night of 3rd May, the pope was in Lusaka and due in Malawi the next morning, Thursday 4th May. On the night of 3rd at about 10.00pm John received a call to go to Party headquarters. When he arrived he was told that the Party was not happy about the visit. The main reason was that the president was not being given enough prominence. When John asked what it was they wanted, they said that they wanted the pope to greet the president on his way to the altar for mass. They wanted the president to do a reading. They wanted the president to be incensed when the pope was being incensed. At the sign of peace they wanted the pope to come down from the podium and greet the president. And when mass was over, the pope, on his way out, should stop by the president and show reverence. Listening with growing disbelief to the list, John reminded the Party officials that the details of the visit had already been agreed with the archbishop in charge, that it was a pastoral visit and could not be politicised in this way.

The argument went on and on and became quite heated. John stood firm and eventually they asked for some compromise. John explained that there could be no compromise. The visit was planned, the security personnel were briefed on the pope's actions, there could be no change. The argument continued. Eventually, approaching midnight and conscious of all that had yet to be done, John told them that the archbishop in charge of the trip was in Lusaka with the pope and they should talk to him. They phoned the archbishop, who asked to speak to John. On taking the receiver, he put the speaker on so that the conversation could be heard by the Party officials. The archbishop laid down the parameters very clearly: either the papal visit takes place as planned or it does not take place at all. With that, John took his leave and returned to the archbishop's (of Malawi) house to finalise all the last minute details. About one hour later, two more Party men appeared at the house with the message that the Party was not happy with the arrangements. At that point, John completely lost his patience and told them if the president did not like the arrangements, he need not come to the mass. If he wanted to come, he would be welcome as a worshipping Christian to pray with the Chief Shepherd of the Catholic people in Malawi.

Though the men departed in no doubt about the protocol, there were several attempts by Party officials to interfere during the mass and to disrupt the protocol during the visit generally. Despite the hours of discussion the night before, as the pope approached the altar, two men ran out and tried to re-direct him towards the president. The Malawian bishops, reluctant to take a public stand against the Party, left John to face them down and prevent the visit being turned into a Party jamboree.

In preparation for the visit, the bishops' conference prepared a number of sermons focussing on matters of justice, peace and human rights. While the pope likes to receive such sermons for his visits, he always retains the right to use them or not as he decides. The conference had chosen four of their number, John among them, to prepare the sermons. The committee was pleased with what they had drawn up. It was unsurprising then that there was a general disappointment among the bishops that the pope chose not to use them in a public forum. However, on Friday, 5th May, he gave a private audience to the bishops at the residence of the Bishop of Blantyre. Towards the end of his address, he said: "*Within the context of evangelisation and formation, the Church is deeply committed to the promotion of the dignity of the human person and the good of society through authentic human development....this means a commitment to justice and peace in collaboration with all who have true human values at heart. As I stated in my encyclical letter Sollicitudo Rei Socialis: 'the condemnation of evils and injustices is also a part of that ministry of evangelisation in the social field which is an aspect of the Church's prophetic role.' ...the Kingdom of God means working for justice, peace and reconciliation.*"[1] For the men listening and for John Roche, in particular, these words were pointing the way

[1] *L'Osservatore Romano, N.22 29th May 1989. p 19.*

towards action and confirmation of tacit approval by the Vatican for any action taken in the cause of human rights and justice. While Pope John Paul II was emphatic in his comments, urging the bishops' conference to take responsibility for prophetic leadership, the bishops were disappointed that he had not made comments in a more public forum. Members of the Catholic community generally were also deeply disappointed that the pope did not make some kind of public statement on matters of justice and human rights. Such an act would have helped to strengthen the bishops' hand in facing the government and the Party machine.

For the Malawian people generally, the visit was a great success. While the visit was primarily a pastoral visit to the Catholic community, the country as a whole entered into the spirit of it. Even the government, despite the problems of protocol, put financial and logistical support in place without which the visit would have been impossible. For the Catholics, particularly the younger people, there was an extraordinary affirmation of their identity. They had a real sense of belonging to something much bigger than what was confined within the borders of Malawi. When the pope made his customary declaration of love for the young people of Malawi, they erupted in a joyous tumult of singing and dancing. Their experience of leadership through government, the police, the Malawi Young Pioneers and the Youth League, was rooted in fear and terror; now here was a leader telling them that they were worth something and that he loved them. The euphoria lifted the oppressed people of Malawi for a while and gave them real joy. For John, the exhaustion was so complete, he did not even have the energy to worry about any Party backlash for his uncompromising stand on the protocol of the visit. He took a certain degree of comfort from the fact that he had faced down the politicians in a public forum and he knew that the people had noticed.

After the visit, John took ten days leave and went to a little cabin by the lake for a complete rest. He was to need all his stamina in the months ahead, for 1989 was a also a significant year in the history of Malawi for an altogether different reason than the visit of the pope.

Msgr. John Roche

Msgr. John Roche meets Pope John Paul II (1989).

The Passover carved by James Chikasasa and James Samikwa.
(Hanging in the Missionary Institute, London)

*Msgr. John Roche and Fr. Mark Mkandwire with Mrs. Luhanga (centre),
her children and her mother. Mrs. Luhanga died shortly afterwards.*

Young girl looking after her sister near Mua.

A girl fetching water in Chimteka.

Two friends near Mua.

A typical dwelling.

Lake Malawi.

A girl doing her laundry near Mua.

A girl carrying maize (cornflour).

A group of children in Mchinji.

A woman fetching water from the well in Chimteka.

Villagers preparing for a celebration in Chimteka.

The local football team at Katete.

Looking across the plains towards the mountains.

Every year His Excellency, the Life President, Ngwasi Dr. H. Kamuzu Banda (he always insisted on being addressed by his full title) used to carry out crop inspections in the country. Despite periodic food shortages that caused great hardship, especially in the central and southern regions, where the bulk of the population lived, these visits were carried out to 'prove' that the government's agricultural policies were a success.

Whenever the president visited an area, people had to line up on the roadside from 6.00am and no excuse was accepted. Even if there was a funeral, it either had to be hurried or delayed so that it would not interfere with the president's visit. The crop that he was to inspect would be identified well in advance and the owner would be given fertilisers so that the crop would look well and show a good yield. Closer to the time of the presidential visit, inspectors would visit the area to view the crops. If the crop in the adjoining fields were of poor quality or unsightly, they were simply levelled. The fact that the owners had worked hard in their fields and needed the crops, both for their own food and as a source of income, was of no consequence.

These crop inspection tours were also a source of gifts and revenue for the president. Every village had to produce a suitable gift, usually of money, but other things could also be included. Businesses, associations, groups and individuals were all levied. Churches were also expected to present some kind of 'gift.' Villages would be told in advance what was acceptable and they had come up with the 'suggested' figure regardless of the circumstances of the villagers. To refuse to contribute was to insult His Excellency, the Life President, Ngwasi, Dr. H. Kamuzu Banda, and to insult the president was to face certain detention.

During one such inspection in 1989, it was reported to the president that in the central region teachers from the north were not respecting the local customs and were favouring outsiders over local boys in the schools. There had been a constant simmering resentment of the northerners since independence. For reasons of history the best education in the country was offered in the north at Livingstonia. As a result, many civil servants, teachers and administrators came from the north. They worked all over the country and were perceived by the people in the other regions as always getting the 'best jobs.' The retention of their own language by the Tumbuka people from the north was also a bone of contention for the others as Chichewa and English were the official languages. The sense of separate identity of the northerners was deeply resented. Also, if there was any questioning of the political status quo, it was more likely to come from the north. The northerners had a very strong sense of identity bound up with culture and language. As a patrilineal society they held the matrilineal societies of the central and south in very low esteem, so the antagonism and resentment flowed both ways. From time to time there were purges of northerners from the civil service and public administration and so the resentment and division was frequently fuelled.

The complaint made to Dr. Banda threw him into a rage and he decreed that all teachers should return to their region of origin. As always when the president spoke, there were those ready to implement his wishes immediately. Teachers were told to pack up and go home. They were not allowed to make orderly arrangements to transport themselves and their goods. A lorry arrived on a given day, it was loaded with whatever could be fitted on and that was that. Anything not loaded when the lorry was ready to go was left behind. Apart from the disruption, this move caused much economic hardship. Teachers were not paid very well and it was usual for them to be given a garden by the local people as a form of payment. They farmed their gardens as a source of extra income. The decree to move back to their region of origin came in the middle of the growing season, and the valuable gardens just had to be abandoned. There were those who objected to being evicted from their homes and jobs, and as a result were very badly beaten. It is known that some even died from the beatings.

Hunting all the northern teachers home to their region of origin had a major impact on the schools of the other regions. Suddenly, they were left with too few qualified teachers. Students who had only just completed secondary school were drafted back in as teachers, so the education of the children of the central and southern regions suffered considerably.

In Mzuzu, trucks were arriving every other day with stunned teachers and their families. There had been no alternative arrangements made for housing or for jobs. The wives of teachers were also victimised; if they wanted to keep the family intact they were also forced to abandon their jobs and professions and move with their husbands to a very uncertain future. If the teacher was a woman, her husband also suffered the same fate. Many families were broken up because of this extraordinary decree.

Apart from the economic implications of this disruption, there were also considerable social problems. A teacher would have had a certain standing within his community particularly in one that was patriarchal and hierarchical. He would have been in a position to support his extended family both through direct financial help and more indirectly through hospitality in his home extended to those attending college or working away from home. Suddenly he had nothing. Overnight, he went from a position of honour and the source of help to his family to being in need of help himself, without a home and a means of support. Many men would have felt deeply shamed by their situation – believing their whole sense of manhood had been called into question.

The Church within the diocese of Mzuzu offered some financial help to displaced teachers, but means were limited. They also encouraged the village communities to receive the teachers with dignity and to help in whatever ways were possible. There were not enough jobs in the northern region to re-employ all the teachers, and there was a very real anger within the people. Trying to find expression for the anger was difficult as it had already been demonstrated with brutal clarity what happened to those who did so. In an attempt to give focus and expression to the huge anger in the north, John Roche brought the matter to the episcopal conference for discussion. While the other bishops were aware of what had happened and were disturbed by it, they had no idea of the terrible human cost involved, as their areas of influence and administration were in the central and southern regions. John argued the case passionately and the bishops were appalled by what they heard. There was a general agreement that the conference should seek a meeting with Dr. Banda to discuss the problem and find a workable solution. It was a catch-phrase of Dr. Banda's that his door was always open and he was always available to his people. For some of the bishops, to agree to this was a major step forward, requiring considerable courage.

A letter seeking an appointment with Dr. Banda was drafted and sent to his office. The bishops were given a date for a meeting, but the date was a continually moveable feast. It was Malawi Congress Party policy to keep a low profile when their actions or those of the president caused a major upheaval. It happened in 1984 following the murders of the ministers: the Young Pioneers and Youth League disappeared off the streets, there were no big MCP events, even the police maintained a low profile. As regional superior in Lilongwe at the time, John experienced the immense anger of the people. Even though the central region was a Malawi Congress Party stronghold, the people were appalled at what had happened to the ministers. In the country since 1972, this was the first time John saw a real, raw anger given expression by the people. They were angry about the killing of the ministers, but incensed at the conduct of their burial, particularly that of Aaron Gadama. The people of Malawi show tremendous respect to the dead. No matter what people did in their lives, when they died, they were buried with respect. A funeral was a community affair to accompany the deceased to their final resting place. When Gadama was being buried, nobody was allowed near the grave. A priest who wished to attend was turned back. A cordon was thrown up about three kilometres from the graveyard. For the people, this was treating the remains of the man no better than one might treat a dog. But there was no leadership to give voice to the anger, not from political life and not from the Church. But despite all, the Party laid low, and without a focus the heat of the people's anger eventually dissipated and things returned to normal.

The government tried a similar strategy with the bishops. After a month's waiting, with the proposed meeting constantly being re-scheduled, the bishops met again to discuss their options. They accepted that either the president did not want to meet them or else the letter had never reached him in the first place. Angered by the lack of response, there was a suggestion that a pastoral letter should be written on the matter as a way of giving voice to the terrible injustice. The idea was well received and there was significant support for it. Unfortunately, the support for a pastoral letter was not unanimous. For a pastoral letter to be published, there would have to be unanimous agreement among the bishops. Though the idea petered out and in the end nothing was done, which only seemed to validate the government's strategy of evasion, nevertheless, that the bishops were thinking of the possibilities of a pastoral letter, regardless of the possible consequences, was a major step forward. Though the pastoral letter would not be written for another two and half years, the tiny seed was sown in 1989.

Early in 1991, John's three-year term of office as apostolic administrator had drawn to a close. He contacted Rome to request his release from office, reminding them that they had signed an agreement with him. Acknowledging the agreement, the authorities in Rome asked John to fill one more year. A problem had arisen with the candidate initially being prepared to succeed him and John was asked to nominate somebody else. The person he had in mind was only eight years ordained and was in Ireland, having been sent there by John to do a course in spirituality and a leadership course in the Milltown Institute and Loreto House respectively. Fr. Joseph Zuza still needed another year to complete his studies in Dublin. So John agreed to spend one more year as apostolic administrator. He consoled himself with the thought that it was only one more year.

— Chapter 10 —
Pastoral letter

As time went on, it was inevitable that things had to change in Malawi. Dr. Banda, who was now in his late eighties or early nineties (depending on which date of birth was accepted), was visibly weakening. His Official Hostess, Mama Kadzamira, and her uncle, John Tembo, who had survived all cabinet and Party purges since independence, were increasingly becoming more visible. There was increasing pressure within Malawi, among the third level students, among the religious and among the laity in general, for the bishops to take a lead. Just before Christmas 1991 some person or group sent anonymous Christmas cards to various commercial companies with the message "Wishing you a happy Christmas and a New Year full of the joys of multiparty democracy." Excited by the prospect of what such a communication could achieve, Fr. Pádraig Ó Máille, with some friends and activists, including the future president of Malawi, Bakili Muluzi, successfully organised a similar letter campaign for Martyrs Day, 3rd March, 1992. They asked questions about the living martyrs, those in detention, those suffering for their work for human rights and those suffering ethnic discrimination.

The Christian Churches of all denominations had remained conspicuously quiet throughout all the years of oppression. The statement of the Blantyre Synod of the Presbyterian Church after the bishops' pastoral letter clearly admits this: "*After Independence the Central Church of the African Presbyterium was aligned closely with the government and became so assimilated with the Government activities that the Synod was often invited to pray and participate as a Church at various government functions. However, because of this assimilation and alignment with the M.C.P.* [Malawi Congress Party] *the Church gradually lost its ability to admonish or speak out pastorally to the government.*"

There is an irony in this as a significant number of the participants of the Chilembwe Rising belonged to the Blantyre Synod, and a significant number of those fighting for independence also belonged to the Blantyre Synod. Recognising its potential as a seedbed for rebellion, Dr. Banda manipulated the Synod to his own purposes from the start, thus neutralising its power to effect change.

Within the Catholic bishops' conference also there was ambivalence about the oppressive actions of the government. Some members would have been politically supportive of the Malawi Congress Party, others would have been lukewarm in their attitude, and others would have been deeply concerned at the legitimising of the terror visited upon the people by their government. Many of the other episcopal conferences in Africa were making important statements on justice and peace, thus challenging the Malawi conference to speak out. For the bishops there was also the echo of the pope's visit and his words to them in their private meeting with him, urging them to be part of a prophetic Church.

Communications had improved greatly and Malawi was no longer as isolated as it had been. People within the country were becoming more aware of what was going on elsewhere and other countries were becoming more aware of Malawi and its oppressive regime. The introduction of multiparty democracy in Zambia, Malawi's neighbour was a source of amazement and great hope to the Malawian people. The fall of communism in Europe was another ray of hope. If unthinkable change could come about elsewhere, surely it could also happen in Malawi. Leaders in villages, towns and cities were beginning to ask questions. Could there be another way to govern? Was there anyone in Malawi prepared to stand up and give voice and vision to the people's questioning?

On 20th January, 1992, the bishops gathered in Lilongwe for their plenary meeting. Present at the meeting were Archbishop James Chiona, Bishops Felix Mkhori, Alessandro Assolari, Alan Chamgwera, Mathias Chimole, Gervasio Chisendera and Apostolic Administrator John Roche. Also present were the Apostolic Pro-Nuncio, Archbishop Leanza, and Fr. Nazarius Mugungwe, Secretary General to the conference.

About three weeks before this meeting, the executive of the episcopal conference met to draw up the agenda. There was nothing unusual about the meeting. The main item on the agenda was the discussion between the delegation of the conference and the government officials on matters of health and education. This had been a very difficult meeting and the prevailing attitude of the government seemed to be that it was the Church's responsibility to come up with finance, but the government had all the administrative control and all that that implied in terms of how people were treated. The school curriculum could be changed and teachers moved around without any consultation. There were ongoing difficulties between Church and state in the administration of schools and hospitals. Issues concerning equality in the wage structure and respect for the ethos of the Church were causing particular tension. By 1992, the Church was providing over 50% of the medical care in the country, yet was only receiving 6% of the health budget.

At the bishops' meeting, the results of the meeting of the health and education delegation with the government were discussed. The bishops were very disappointed at the lack of progress and at the intractable attitude of the government, because for them, health and education were central to their mission and leadership. They considered the matter and wondered what the next step should be. It was then that Archbishop Chiona, chairman of the episcopal conference, calmly proposed that a pastoral letter be written to deal with this and other issues of human rights and good governance. This idea was taken up immediately by all the bishops and this time there was complete unanimity among them. There was some discussion about approaching some of the other Christian Churches to come on board, but at that time there was little or no relationship between the various churches. Also, the wider the consultation, the greater risk of a leak to the authorities. In the end it was decided to contain the matter within the conference to ensure the best chance of success. Even the Catholic priests of the country would not get to hear of the letter until three or four days before it was due to be read out.

All other matters were put to one side and the rest of the day was taken up with discussion on the format and content of the letter. The main business, that of the content of the letter and the choice of the drafting committee, was completed by lunchtime. The rest of the day was taken up with fine-tuning the ideas. It was decided that the letter would be read out at all Masses on the first Sunday of Lent, which in 1992 fell on 8th March.

A drafting committee of six people was proposed. Great care was taken in choosing the six people, they had to have theological competence and be wholly trustworthy so that no whisper of the letter would leak out. In considering names of likely people, John Roche expected that his confrère, Fr. Pádraig Ó Máille would be a possible candidate. The bishops, however, were concerned that, given his involvement with the students, his clandestine activities supporting detainees and his noted opposition to the regime he was likely to be under particular scrutiny by the security forces. They could not take any risk that the security forces would discover their plan to issue a letter.

Six people were chosen and included Malawians and expatriates. [Ten years on, it is still advisable to keep the names of the committee secret]. John Roche was asked to chair the committee. There were two reasons for this: he was competent in English and had some practice in writing other material on behalf of the conference. It is also possible that some of bishops felt safer with an expatriate chairing the committee if things were to go drastically wrong.

John Roche had no misgivings about accepting the chairmanship of the drafting committee. For him there was a very strong sense of 'at last, we the leaders are leading.' In the days following the bishops' meeting John contacted each of the proposed names, inviting them to a meeting in Lilongwe. He gave no indication whatsoever of the agenda of the meeting except to indicate that it was at the invitation of the bishops. Before the week was out, the six members and John met in Lilongwe. He explained what the bishops had in mind and after a moment's stunned silence one of the men present spoke for all of them: "thanks be to God, at last!" Full of joy and energy they set to work immediately. Procedures were discussed and it was agreed that those who lived near each other could work together, but others were to work singly, so that suspicions would not be aroused – confidentiality was essential. John laid out the matters that the bishops wanted to discuss and in no time at all they had divided up the areas of discussion between the six people. They had agreed that each would work on a specific area while keeping the unity of the letter in mind. Energised and excited, each went their own way, conscious of the great honour and great burden it was to be involved in the making of history.

Two weeks later they reconvened on the set date, Friday 14th February, in Lilongwe. Each person had done an incredible amount of work and the day was spent in considering the content and general editing - each line of text had to be considered in all its implications. When he complimented them on their fine work, one priest replied to John: "it was relatively easy, it was if it had been lying somewhere deep within waiting to be called forth." This second meeting of the drafting committee was also its final meeting. Over the weekend, two of the priests and John worked on bringing the sections of the letter together to create a single document. When all of that had been done, John then wrote the introduction to the letter. Not to arouse suspicions, they went to the seminary in Zomba where it would not be unusual for such group to be together and where they had easy access to computers. By Sunday evening, as they went their separate ways, they had a coherent document prepared for presentation to the bishops at their emergency meeting to be held the next day, Monday, 17th February. Reading over what they had produced and realising its radical nature, they hoped and prayed that the bishops would have the courage to accept it.

Back in Lilongwe on Sunday evening, as he contemplated the work of the committee, John felt the shame of twenty years of silence lift from his soul. His only fear now was that when they read the document, the bishops might draw back from the brink. They had come further than they ever had before, but they yet had to make that final leap of faith into the darkness.

The following evening the bishops met at the archbishop's house in Lilongwe. After supper, the draft was produced and John gave a report on the workings of the drafting committee. Archbishop Chiona asked that each of the members would take a copy of the draft and spend the rest of the evening alone as they considered it. He wanted no discussion until the document had been fully internalised by all present. They would reconvene at 8.00am the next morning to discuss it. John spent an uneasy night hoping and praying that the bishops would not lose courage. Whatever the bishops decided, for him there could be no going back.

The next morning as they sat down, Archbishop Chiona immediately praised the 'excellent' document. As the archbishop was extremely influential within the conference, as leader his approbation was critical. He said there was no need to read it through as a group. Even this was an extraordinary statement, for, as previous experience of meetings had shown, the archbishop had the capacity to listen for hours to endless discussion. They had all read it individually and if there were any clarifications needed, they could be discussed. There were a few minor queries that were quickly sorted. On the whole the comments were affirming: that it was a well-written document, containing truths that badly needed to be stated. During their discussions one of the bishops suggested that the insertion of some of their proverbs would be useful. Proverbs were an integral part of the cultural wisdom in the various ethnic groups and were frequently used to illustrate important truths.

By the time they were finished, the document had become their pastoral letter and was truly a collective effort. All the bishops were enthused by it. There had been some concern about one or two of the men and how they might accept it. There was one bishop in particular, a senior bishop, who was always called to Party functions and always seemed happy to oblige. He usually attended in full regalia, and while some of the bishops may have felt embarrassment, they all remained silent about his involvement. But even he was totally behind the letter and all it had to say. The atmosphere was electric and John knew with certainty that there was no going back. The bishops were going to make their stand. In discussing possible government reaction, the bishops decided that an attack on one bishop would be an attack on all. They would maintain solidarity and demand that all were treated the same. This should ensure resistance to the government's well-recognised 'divide and conquer' tactics.

The next big concern was printing the pastoral letter. The diocesan press, Likuni, was suggested by one bishop, but given the concerns about Party infiltration of all businesses, this was ruled out by another. While the religious brother in charge was wholly reliable, it had to be assumed that there was a government informer planted among the lay staff who were in the majority. Having come this far, they could not risk being discovered and out-manoeuvred, or worse, by the Party. Someone suggested that they should approach Balaka Press in Mangochi owned by the Montfort Fathers. It was operated by Fr. Pierre Gamba an Italian priest. The bishops were confident that Fr. Gamba could guarantee total confidentiality and security. John Roche was delegated to contact Fr. Gamba and explain the situation. Before their meeting concluded, the bishops decided that work on translation of the pastoral letter into Chitumbuka and Chichewa should begin straight away, so that it would be ready for reading at all masses in all the parishes on Sunday 8th March.

Following the bishops' meeting, some small adjustments to the letter were necessary and the proverbs had to be included, so John took the text back to the seminary in Zomba to make the alterations. From Zomba he telephoned Fr. Gamba in Mangochi and arranged to meet him at the Press with two other members of the drafting committee on Wednesday, 19th February. Fr. Gamba was ecstatic when he heard what he was being asked to print. He asked to be allowed to share the secret with one of the congregation's religious brothers. He guaranteed confidentiality by promising to do the actual printing himself with help from the brother. He also promised that the translations would be ready if he received them in time. Fr. Gamba gave no thought to the possible repercussions for himself, for the Balaka Press or its building.

The translations were with the printers on time and all printing was completed by Sunday, 1st March. The packages were collected from Balaka Press and transported by car to the various diocesan centres. This was one of two points of weakness in the whole production and had been a source of worry. But collection and distribution passed off safely. The bishops had decided to call their diocesan clergy together midweek to explain the letter and distribute copies for reading at the Mass on Sunday. This was the second point of weakness. As much as they might emphasise the importance of confidentiality, once they had made the letter known to the priests there was a greater risk that it would leak out through excitement.

Matters were complicated further by a standard courtesy visit to Dr. Banda which had been arranged for Wednesday, 4th March. Delegations from other groups and interests in the country were also scheduled for the same day.

These types of visit were not unusual and were part and parcel of the Party propaganda machine. They were designed to make it appear that the President was listening to the people by meeting their representatives. The bishops could not cancel the meeting and raise suspicions. This particular meeting was to introduce Fr. Tarcisius Ziyaye who had been nominated by Pope John Paul II as the Auxiliary Bishop of Dedza. The report in the *Daily Times* the next day had a headline: *Church, State in partnership* and went on to describe in glowing terms how the Church and the State '*are partners and not rivals in looking after interests of the people.*'

Despite all the efforts to maintain secrecy, there was almost a disaster when one of John's own confrères who worked in a diocese in the south read the letter out ahead of time. He was given the box of letters from the diocesan centre without any instruction. Whereas most of the parishes were having the Lenten Ash service on Sunday 8th March, his was a day or two earlier. Luckily, for whatever reason, there was no particular reaction to it. However, John, who was now back in Mzuzu, received a call on Friday, 6th March, from a friend in Zomba who heard a rumour that Sunday was going to be a big day, that something was going to be read out. He was absolutely terrified. To have managed to get this far and be stymied at the last moment was almost too much to bear. He wanted the letter to have the explosive effect that he knew it would have if they could only manage to get safely to Sunday.

In Mzuzu diocese John called the priests together on Thursday 5th March and explained the letter. Just as with the drafting committee, the bishops and Fr. Gamba, the diocesan priests, both indigenous and expatriate, were thrilled with the letter. They praised the content and applauded the bishops. However, there was some concern expressed and John was asked if he and the bishops had put in place any contingency plans for their own safety. He had to admit that apart from their 'attack on one was an attack on all' solidarity, no practical arrangements had been put in place for their safety once the letter was publicly released. However, he had great faith in the reception of the document by the people and that would create its own momentum. The contents of the letter were in accordance with the gospel and therefore should be proclaimed by the priests. The priests, reassured by John's confidence, professed their delight once again in the letter and promised to maintain the embargo on its contents until Sunday morning.

When the priests had left, for the first time John began to think about the consequences of the letter. Knowing the country, the Party and the government as well as he did, the concerns of the priests unsettled him a little. The excitement and pressure of producing multiple printed copies in three languages of a letter that had only been mooted five weeks previously had meant there was very little time to consider the fall-out. When he received the phone call from his friend in Zomba the next afternoon, the worry of a pre-emptive strike against the letter by the government put all thoughts of personal safety out of his mind. All through the rest of Friday and all day Saturday the tension mounted as he dreaded taking the phone call that would tell him the worst had happened. However, there was no Party reaction. It would seem unlikely that nobody from the Party was aware of the premature reading of the letter and the general air of excitement and expectation in the south of the country. Given the omnipresence of Party spies and informers, as well as those who were convinced of the Party's authority to rule, it is very surprising that nothing happened.

Saturday passed almost without incident. In the evening, however, a member of the Church called to the bishop's house and asked what was happening the next day; he had heard it was going to be a 'significant day'. John merely suggested that he wait and see. But again the visitor's words were reason to worry. His brother was politically connected and if this man knew, chances were high that his brother knew. If his brother knew, who else knew? The fact that Kamuzu Banda was visiting the northern region did not help. To have come so far, it was unbearable to think that something might happen at the last minute to prevent the proclamation of the letter. Saturday night did not offer much peace or sleep.

John rose at 5.30am on the morning of Sunday, 8th March, 1992. The day dawned bright and clear. March is right in the middle of the rainy season in Malawi and can be a very wet month, but this Sunday was clear and sunny. He took a walk around the compound trying to focus on the day ahead, praying for courage and guidance. The bishops had all agreed to read the letter in their cathedral parishes. John's first mass was at 8.30am in the Cathedral of St. Peter, which held about 300 people. It was in English and would be attended by many people from the other regions who worked in the north and who did not speak Chitumbuka. There would also be civil servants, senior policemen, people who worked in banks and other offices, and a number of expatriates at the English mass. He could only wonder what their reaction might be.

Everything went as normal up to the time of the homily. Instead of preaching a homily, John read the letter. There was a shocked silence. As he continued reading, he felt the tenor of the silence change from shock to rejection. Becoming more tense as he sensed the shock and hostility, John felt his mouth go dry, but he was determined to proceed to the end. He had waited almost twenty years for this moment, and he was going to have his say. When he had finished, there was no reaction, a most untypical response. Then one or two expatriates clapped, but their effort was lost in the cavernous silence. Mass continued in a leaden atmosphere right to the end.

After mass, John waited outside the cathedral as usual to greet parishioners. Some people avoided him and hurried away. For some, the emotion would have been shock that the church should make such a proclamation that caused them to hurry away, for others it was fear. With the reading of the letter mass had gone on longer than usual, so there was very little time between the end of the 8.30am mass and the beginning of the 10.00am mass to think about the reaction. Having had barely enough time to grab a quick cup of coffee, John headed back to the cathedral for the next mass which was celebrated in Chitumbuka, the local language. It was normally well attended and would be a good barometer of how the letter was going to be received generally. As he approached the church, John was aware of glances and comments. As usual news had got around with amazing speed. The church was full to overflowing, not just with its own members, but there were those from other denominations there also.

As at the earlier mass, the proclamation of the letter replaced the homily. As before, the initial reaction was a shocked silence. But this silence had a different quality altogether, it was neither hostile nor especially positive. There was bound to be shock that such things about human rights and good governance would be spoken of in such a public manner. When about one third of the letter had been read, there was a perceptible shift in the reaction of the congregation. There was a sense of acceptance. John paused for a moment and considered the length of the letter. He asked if he should continue to read, one woman stood and said "Yayi, makani ngawemi! – This is good news!" And it was clear that this congregation wanted to hear every word of the 'good news.' The courage of the woman unlocked the emotions for everyone else. She spoke up in spite of the fact that there was a considerable police presence in the church. The letter was read in its entirety and when it was finished, the women ululated, people clapped and were dancing in the pews. It was to be a reaction seen repeated over the next week or two – initial disbelief and fear, leading to acceptance with a great sense of joy and freedom. Mass was normally a celebratory occasion, particularly the mass in Chitumbuka. On this Sunday there was an added dimension of celebration as it continued.

After mass, people crowded around looking for copies of the letter. There were complaints that there were not enough copies to go around, and arrangements were made to collect extra copies at the bishop's house the next day. When the crowd had dispersed, John went home to his house at Katoto and spent a quiet afternoon. The intensity of the preparation with the added worry of maintaining secrecy had had its effect and that Sunday afternoon was almost anti-climactic as exhaustion took its toll. There were some telephone calls in the afternoon, two or three just saying 'thank you' and no more, no name or identification. One caller rang to say he did not agree with the letter and hung up. Another unidentified voice said "Mwati tsegulira ku khosi" (You have opened our throats). There were calls from a number of the priests who were very excited about it. John contacted one of the other bishops who reported that the letter had gone down very well within his diocese also. It was hardly a surprise that it had been accepted in Mzuzu, but it was heartening to hear that it had gone down well in the other regions as well. There were some dissenting voices among the clergy, though, with three parishes in the central region refusing to read it.

—— Chapter 11 ——

Reaction

International reaction was swift. By 6.30pm on Sunday evening, the BBC World Service phoned Mzuzu diocese looking for a comment. John was more than a little shocked to know that not only had they heard about the pastoral letter so soon, but that he should have been immediately identified as someone who would comment. The only copies of the letter sent out of the country prior to its reading were those to the Vatican and to the pronuncio in Lusaka. Later John discovered that some priests and other groups had got the letter out to sympathetic friends outside the country during the day on Sunday. He did not want to make any public comment, certainly not in an international forum, before the bishops had come together to discuss the popular reaction to the letter. Also, as the most junior member of the episcopal conference, it was not his place to presume the title of spokesman; so he refused to take the call from the BBC, a wise decision as it subsequently turned out.

That he should be concerned about reactions to the letter began to sink in later in the evening, when a number of priests and sisters called. Even though they did not articulate their worries, their congratulations and excitement being the most obvious emotion, their very presence was a statement in itself. If one or two had come, it would not have been remarkable, but when seven or eight arrived, the underlying message was one of concern about what lay ahead. And yet for John there was no real worry. He was still energised and excited by the reception of the pastoral letter by the community. "Yayi, makani ngawemi." It was indeed very good news.

On the morning of Monday, 9th March, around 9.00am the Presbyterian leader called to the bishop's house to congratulate John and the other bishops on their letter, *Living Our Faith*. It was the first time that he, the leader of the biggest denominational group in the north, had crossed the threshold of the bishop's house. That fact that he walked up to the front door in broad daylight in his clerical garb was significant. He was not afraid of being seen by possible watchers. He was generous in his praise of the letter and told John that he had managed to get his hands on a copy and had shared it with his congregation. He requested as many copies as John could give him. His parting words were: "This is truth. Thank you for it."

Given the sad history of ecumenism in Malawi up to that time, this was a ground-breaking move and one very much appreciated by John Roche, both personally and as a leader within the Catholic Church. It was a statement of solidarity that was to be repeated again and again by members of other Christian denominations and also the Islamic community. The chains of denominational exclusivity had been broken and the Churches, including the Catholic Church, that had sinned by their silence were given a new voice.

Around 10.00am on Monday, in between congratulatory phone calls and visits, word came from Lilongwe that the episcopal conference had been summoned to a meeting with the inspector general of police at 9.00am the following morning, Tuesday, at the archbishop's residence in Blantyre. The idea of a meeting was not unduly worrying for John, wondering as he did whether it was likely to be the beginnings of a dialogue. He was a little surprised that the meeting was with the inspector general. He would have expected to be called first to a meeting with the regional inspector of police, who lived in Mzuzu. Later in the morning a friend from Lilongwe phoned to ask what had been written as the photocopier in his office was 'red hot' with people making copies of *Living Our Faith* all morning.

Just before he departed to Lilongwe on the first leg of the journey, John received a disturbing phone call. He was told not to travel alone to the capital, to bring at least two cars. He was quite shocked by the implications of such a warning. Suddenly the question his priests asked when he presented the letter to them came into clearer focus: had the bishops made any contingency plans? That the meeting with the police was possibly the opening of a new dialogue suddenly seemed a rather naïve aspiration. As it happened, the journey to Lilongwe was without incident. At Lilongwe, John met with the secretary general of the episcopal conference, Fr. Nazarius Mugungwe, and they travelled together on to Blantyre. During the journey, they listened to the radio for any reaction to the letter. There was coverage of the president's rally in Mzimba in the north. During the speeches there were strong attacks made on the letter by a number of people. What was most shocking was that the minister for the north, Malani Lungu, made a blistering attack, not only on the letter, but on John Roche personally. Less than 48 hours after the first reading of the pastoral letter and already the expatriate was being scapegoated. In typical Dr. Banda style, the 'divide and conquer' strategy was immediately kicking in. John was isolated and portrayed as a rebel Irishman trying to stir up trouble in peaceful Malawi for his own nefarious purposes. The venom of the attacks was quite shocking. The letter which was the combined effort of the seven members of the episcopal conference and the six-member drafting committee was suddenly, by government sleight-of-hand, becoming the brainchild of just one man: Monsignor John Roche the troublemaker, the expatriate, the rebel Irishman in cahoots with the IRA. The tactic was quite successful in that in the international reportage, *Living Our Faith* was immediately presented as John Roche's pastoral letter, a fact which caused John more than a little embarrassment, and one which he endeavoured to correct at every opportunity.

In Blantyre, there was a great sense of solidarity in meeting the other bishops. The atmosphere was enthusiastic and alive with marvellous stories from each diocese of the acceptance of the letter. In Lilongwe, a Malawi Congress Party member had heard about the letter and approached the bishop before mass to find out if what people were saying was true. The bishop confirmed the Party man's worst expectations and left him in total shock. Given the previous history of the acquiescence of the bishops' conference to the government and the Party, this empowerment to face down the Party was extraordinary. As stories such as these were swapped, the telephone rang with a message that the meeting with the chief of police was being changed from 9.00am to 10.00am and the location was changed from the archbishop's house to the police headquarters.

This news was less than welcome and definitely wrought a change in the atmosphere in the house. The high spirits of the evening were brought to a sober conclusion. The bishops considered their strategy for the next day. It was agreed that whatever happened to one bishop would happen to all. If one were imprisoned, they would all have to be imprisoned. They would insist on their right as religious leaders to speak to their congregations. It was decided that the conference would speak with one voice, and the archbishop was chosen to be the spokesman. He was the obvious choice as the leader of the Catholic Church in Malawi; he was also the chairman of the conference. One of the bishops suggested than John keep as low a profile as possible and to say nothing the next day as he had already been singled out. The warning only served to make John even more uneasy and he spent another wakeful night wondering about his fate, which seemed yet again to be held firmly in someone else's grasp.

As they drove up to the police headquarters the next day, the bishops saw a number of men by the gate, about twelve in all. The men stood there quietly, all wearing rosary beads around their necks. The rosary was to become a symbol of solidarity with the bishops and their letter over the coming weeks. It was worn by Catholics and non-Catholics alike as a symbol of truth and of witness. The silent, dignified protest by the men at the police headquarters was extraordinarily significant. They were making a public stance at the very gates of the institution that upheld and enforced the repressive laws of the government.

The bishops were shown into a large hall with tables and chairs set out for them. Also present were between sixteen and twenty senior policemen from all parts of the country. The inspector general, a Catholic, addressed the bishops indicating his shock and horror that such a document was issued by the Church. He spoke of the letter in terms of treason and sedition. He spoke at length and it became clear that as a member of the Church, he was both protecting his own position and asserting the Party line. He said, "I, as a Catholic cannot understand why you, the leaders of the Church, have taken this most unacceptable step. Kamuzu and the Party have always listened to the Church and respected its autonomy and position." The use of the words 'treason' and 'sedition' were immediately worrying for the bishops. That the discussion should have been catapulted to the national stage so soon was surprise enough, but to hear these words and all they connoted was deeply disturbing. The inspector then played a recording of an interview by the BBC with Trevor Cullen of the Montfort Fathers. The reason for the high-level meeting became obvious. The international media had got hold of the story and was nipping at Dr. Banda's Achilles' heel. Dr. Banda's need for acceptance and respect by international governments bordered on the pathological and now because of this 'troublesome' group of bishops, the uncomfortable truth about Malawi and H. Kamuzu Banda's repressive regime was being revealed in a public way at a high level. When the interview was played, the inspector said that it was proof that the letter had been written in agreement with Malawi's enemies outside the country.

Listening to the recorded interview that had been given by Trevor Cullen, who had spent some time in Malawi, but was in Britain at the time of the letter, John breathed a sigh of relief that he had not responded to the BBC request for an interview on the previous Sunday evening. The fact that he was already being isolated and blamed as the instigator of the letter meant the government would have used any 'evidence' against him, no matter how tenuous.

When he eventually finished his tirade against the bishops and their 'seditious' and 'treasonable' document, the inspector general demanded a response. He refused to allow Archbishop Chiona speak for the conference and looked for a response from each individual bishop. Prepared for this eventuality, the bishops responded to a format: the pastoral letter was part of their responsibility as leaders to educate the faithful on the social teachings of the Church and show how they might be lived out and witnessed to in the Malawi of 1992. In doing this, the bishops were doing no more than following the example of many previous popes and bishops.

John was near the end of the line and felt that when he spoke there was a lot of attention focussed on him. He said as little as possible, merely repeating what had been said by the others before him. One of the bishops asked that they be shown the treasonous parts of the pastoral letter. This led to a tortuous reading of the whole document line by line by one of the administrative assistants who had very poor English. From time to time, the bishops were asked what they meant by a particular sentence or phrase. More often than not, their response was: 'exactly what is written there!' For John, listening to the document being read, albeit badly, with different emphasis was an interesting experience. He was hearing it in an altogether new way and its radical nature was becoming ever more apparent.

The meeting dragged on until 7.00pm with a short break for food. Eventually the bishops were released and they returned to the archbishop's house. Drained and exhausted, during their evening meal they had little to say to one another apart from the occasional feeble joke and nervous laughter. Bishop Assolari decided that he was heading home for the night. He lived about an hour and a half away by car. The others tried to dissuade him, conscious as they were of the highly political nature of the meeting with the inspector general. There were very real concerns about their safety now that sedition and treason had entered the vocabulary of discussion. However, the bishop went home alone regardless of the warnings and arrived safely.

The action of the bishop of Mangochi was well understood by all the men. They all felt that they needed to be in their home place. They were leaders of their community and had spoken as representatives of that community; now if there were to be repercussions, it was important that they be identified with their respective communities. The next morning the bishops dispersed and headed home. John had decided to fly back to Mzuzu as he had not come on to Blantyre in his own car. At the airport he had a strong sense of being watched. While he was waiting for his flight, an expatriate, a man he knew, came up to him and congratulated him on the letter, but could not resist stating the obvious in saying: "Well done, John. But I'm sure you know that the shit has really hit the fan on this one!" Later, a young Malawian man wearing a rosary beads around his neck approached him. John, wearing his clerical garb, was easily identified, and as one of only two expatriate bishops would have been reasonably well-known in the country. The Malawian spoke to him in public, congratulating him on the letter and saying that even though he was not a Catholic, he was wearing the rosary as a gesture of solidarity and thanks. That the man could courageously approach John in a public area, was a source of great joy to him. Further proof for John that the truth of the letter was indeed setting the people free.

An announcement was made that the flight to Lilongwe was delayed which meant that John would miss the onward connection to Mzuzu and would be delayed for a day in Lilongwe. So when he arrived in the capital, he decided to spend the day in the Society's regional centre. After lunch he called on the European Union delegate, Mr. Hugh Johnson. They had known each other well when John was regional superior and had shared many conversations. He was likely to know something of the political manoeuvrings in the city.

Though delighted with the letter, what Mr. Johnson had to say was of small comfort. The Party was having an important meeting that afternoon with delegates coming from all over the country and their mood was anything but conciliatory. He went on to say that John should be concerned about his personal safety and to make sure that someone knew at all times where he was. He used a phrase that was to be repeated many times over the next few days: 'be careful, we know these people, we know what they are capable of.' Though agreeing to take care, privately John felt that Hugh Johnson was exaggerating the situation and over-reacting. He headed back to the regional centre. As he drove back, the need and great desire to be back in Mzuzu surfaced again, it was almost like a call. Given the Party attitude, John was deeply concerned at what might be happening in the north, especially to the priests.

Back at the regional centre, Paddy Hagan, then regional superior, called to John's room with a disturbing message. Hugh Johnson had telephoned to say that John was to get over to the EU delegate's house without delay. Not only that, but he was not, under any circumstances, to travel in his own car. Paddy Hagan took him over there immediately. Johnson was waiting at the door when they arrived. John was hurried into the house, out of sight. In the short time between John's visit to him and this summons to his home, the EU delegate had received information from the Party meeting. Those attending the meeting were furious at the letter and the bishops. During their angry deliberations a decision had been taken to kill all the signatories of the letter and that the punishment was to be carried out immediately.

─── Chapter 12 ───
Death Threats

That the decision to kill the bishops was not just Party rhetoric was proved conclusively even as Hugh Johnson was in the process of telling John the news. While they were talking, they heard a car skid to a halt outside. Johnson immediately ordered John to go into a back room and to stay out of sight. Hardly understanding what was happening, John complied. As the front door opened he heard his name mentioned. A few moments later, the British Ambassador entered the back room with the words, "John, am I happy to see you!" The ambassador had received a similar report to Johnson of the Party meeting, but from a different source. He had also heard that John Roche had been specifically targeted among the bishops and was to be killed on his way back to Mzuzu. About half way along the Mzuzu road from Lilongwe there was a police roadblock, ostensibly to deter those who would cut down trees illegally and steal the timber. Everybody heading north had to stop at this roadblock. If he were to have the misfortune to have a 'car accident' this would be the ideal spot to be picked up and despatched.

Given the high-level concern for his safety, John could not dismiss the death threats as idle rumour. The threats raised the stakes considerably. While not giving much thought to the possible repercussions of the letter, John knew there was always the possibility of violence of some sort, but had never considered the ultimate violence of murder. He had thought of imprisonment, expulsion (the usual fate of non-compliant expatriates) or possibly a severe beating by the Young Pioneers, who, if given the green light, would have been happy to oblige. To face the possibility that someone willed his death for speaking nothing more than the truth was a truly terrifying experience. That was something that he had not considered on any level before now. Though the room was busy with the urgent conversation of the three other men present, for John they did not exist; his world had been reduced to a silent conversation between himself and death. Facing the possibility of his death left John with the powerful feeling that whatever he might have to face, he was not yet ready for this. He was only forty-four years old, and had just spoken out in the very public way he had wanted to over the twenty years of his missionary work. This was meant to be a new beginning not the end of everything. He sat alone, numb with shock and fear, unable to react in any way.

Hugh Johnson insisted that John stay with him and his wife Danielle; that way there was some hope of protection. John was discouraged from standing at a window or an open door. He could not go out into the garden. This led to some speculation in the country that he had been placed under house arrest. Later he recorded in his diary: "Heard of the death threats today. Can people be so mad! Fear is like a raw and biting presence in my heart and body."

Given the seriousness of the death threat, Johnson suggested that the pronuncio in Lusaka be informed and encouraged to come to Malawi to offer diplomatic support. A diplomat, he knew it was necessary to internationalise the situation in order to gain some protection for the bishops. This was agreed and a telephone call was made to Lusaka

Another difficult night was endured - these were becoming uncomfortably common. The next morning, Hugh Johnson arrived with the newspapers. Only one viewpoint could be expected, as the newspapers were owned by Banda's company, Press Holdings Ltd. Sure enough, the reports on the bishops' letter were scathing. It did not help that the bishops had attended the meeting with Dr. Banda only four days before the proclamation of the letter. The glowing reports following this meeting of the co-operation between Church and State now only served to make the government look ridiculous.

In the Daily Times of Friday, 13th March, 1992 the bishops were lambasted. As every meeting with, and speech by, the president was usually recorded and broadcast by the Malawi Broadcasting Corporation (also part of the Press Holdings empire), the formulaic speech given by Archbishop Chiona praising the leadership of Dr. Banda was replayed at the Party meeting. That the speech could not be otherwise – detention was the sword of Damocles that hung over any utterance to do with the president - was conveniently overlooked. The newspaper reported that: '*This is therefore a clear case of deceit and double standards which has aroused anger throughout the whole country.*' The report went on to say: '*Delegates therefore resolved to condemn unreservedly the attempt by the bishops to expropriate the Catholic Church to enter politics and use the pulpit to sow seeds of confusion... and to disturb the peace, stability, progress and hard won freedom which has been achieved under the wise and dynamic leadership of the Ngwasi. Furthermore, delegates were left in no doubt whatsoever of the lies, hypocrisy and double-facedness of the bishops who until now have presented an innocent face of gratitude...when they had on their own manufactured and harboured a diabolical scheme to introduce another Christian Liberation Party* [former opposition party] *in different guise.*'

Further reports in the newspaper record Dr. Banda's own address to the Party meeting. It displayed his usual tactic of divide and conquer. This time it was a two-pronged attack. He attempted to isolate the bishops from the people by saying he '*was happy that ordinary Catholics were behind their country and not the bishops*' and isolate John Roche from the bishops when John was mentioned specifically as having drafted the pastoral letter, by saying '*as an Elder of the Church of Scotland he was not surprised* [that John was involved] *since the Catholics in Dublin, Ireland, did not like the Presbyterians in Scotland.*' The isolation and scapegoating of the Irish expatriate continued in both the print and broadcast media, with ever-increasing virulence.

Having read and listened to all that was being said about him, John realised that now his death was a very real possibility and that he needed to consider the implications of this and actively make some choices. The numbing shock of the previous day had passed and he now wished to take some control of what was happening to him. He needed somebody to accompany him on this inner journey and telephoned Paddy Hagan, the regional superior, and asked him to call over.

Paddy sat and listened to John as he talked about what was happening to him. He asked occasional clarifying questions, but mainly listened as John moved from fear, loneliness, darkness and the nadir of his possible death to a new awakening of hope and trust and an inner peace wherein he felt the certainty of a presence take his hand and lead him out of the darkness where he let go all securities, ambitions and desires. He entered this moment of total vulnerability and surrender, and through that arrived at an abiding sense of peace and tranquillity. He had accepted that if death was the price for proclaiming the 'Good News', it was a price he was willing to pay. For John, the 'God of Surprises' who had accompanied him through his ministry came to him at this, his Calvary moment, and breathed new life, new hope into him, blessing him with complete acceptance of whatever would come his way.

Several other things happened that same Friday. The inspector general of the police met with the chairpersons and secretaries of all the parish councils in the country at the police headquarters in Blantyre. It was a tactic to intimidate the people and separate them from the bishops. Though the parish councils were run by the laity, technically the parish priests were the chairmen of the councils. So instead of a large group of lay people who through family ties had a lot to lose if they stood their ground, the police were faced with a group made up mostly of priests, containing a significant number of expatriate missionary members and a number of lay people.

When the priests and lay members entered, the four walls were lined with policemen. Nobody was allowed speak. The chairmen were harangued by the inspector and told to inform their faithful on the next Sunday that the pastoral letter was subversive and a pack of lies. The secretary general of the episcopal conference who attended the meeting asked if the Church could not dialogue with the authorities on the situation and was promptly detained for his impertinence, but released a short time later. No further action was taken and none of the priests withdrew the message of the letter on the following Sunday.

The solidarity of the priests with their bishops was not echoed by actions of the pro-nuncio. He did not come to Malawi in person, but sent his secretary, Msgr. Castro. The diplomats protecting John were astounded. Given the seriousness of the situation, and understanding the African context, it seemed diplomatically gauche to say the least, for the pro-nuncio to send his secretary. In a strongly hierarchical society the absence of the pro-nuncio would have been interpreted in a negative way. It could have been considered a snub to the Malawian government that the pro-nuncio chose to send in his secretary, or else that the bishops really did not have the support of the wider Church for their actions. Either way, the pro-nuncio's lack of presence impinged negatively on how the government viewed the bishops. Despite Msgr Castro's ability and undoubted diplomatic skills, he would have been viewed by the government as very much the 'junior' man – the messenger boy, as it were. Therefore, in their eyes, John and his fellow bishops were not perceived as important enough to warrant their local 'chief' coming to Malawi and looking after their interests. In the hierarchical context, meeting at a level of equality ensured mutual respect for position and also allowed the possibility of hard discussion and tough negotiation. A 'minion' is not mandated to speak for the 'paramount chief.' This lack of public solidarity could only confirm the government in their plans to undermine the bishops in whatever way they could.

The attacks in the media continued. Listening to the constant barrage of negative comment, John found that he was beginning to doubt himself and the action the bishops had taken. He began to realise the powerful psychology behind the idea that if you keep telling somebody they are bad and that they are wrong they will eventually begin to doubt themselves. That he could begin to doubt the wisdom of the proclamation of the letter, knowing how well it was received only five days after the event, pointed to the well-practised manipulative power of the government.

While at the official level the Church may have let the bishops down in their moment of trial and fear, other people buoyed them up by wholehearted support. The care and attention of the British Ambassador and also the EU delegate and his wife who kept John in their home to protect him was a very humbling experience for him. Faxes from all over the world started appearing. Through the BBC World Service, the plight of the bishops was brought into the international spotlight immediately. The World Service kept up a stream of reports on what was happening inside the country. A copy of the recording of the Malawi Congress Party meeting was smuggled out to the BBC. It was translated and broadcast on the World Service. Both men and women were equally trenchant in their denouncing of the bishops at the meeting. Some of the milder extracts were:

1. The one mentioned, the white man from Mzuzu, cannot pass/will not pass the Dwangwa [a river]. It is finished!
2. The seven bishops, we don't want to see here in Malawi. Wherever they go, the people will kill them.
3. Those seven people, I won't mention bishops - *a pite*. [Let them go. Die!]
4. Anyone who questions Ngwasi cannot stay alive. *Saonekera!* [They are not to be seen again!]

Access to the foreign media was possible through the use of the fax machine. People within Malawi were able to get news out every day to have it reported internationally. The government tried to block the fax machines and while it had some success, it could not interfere with all the machines, particularly those of businesses, so the steady flow of news continued.

The fax was equally important for getting information into the country as well. Support flowed in from other bishops' conferences in Africa and from conferences in other countries around the world as well as other international groups and organisations. All this support was a welcome antidote to the vituperation poured out in the newspapers and the radio. A letter written on 13th March by the University of Malawi Catholic Students Association began "*Our beloved bishops,*" and named each in turn: "*From time immemorial a people of God, the people of Malawi, have only heard of independence, freedom from the colonial oppression without actually enjoying the claimed freedom. They have contained within themselves grief and anguish. They did not have a mouth with which to speak these out. ...At long last the moment we all impatiently awaited has come. ...The pastoral letter of yours to us, Catholics, has been very much appreciated and supported by all, for it has been a mouthpiece for the voiceless and powerless and is a clear indication of care for the poor and the oppressed. ...We are fully aware of what it means to say the truth, and this has been manifested in all the noise that has followed your inspired pastoral letter. We commend your boldness in this venture. The insults that have come to you have also reached us. Some misguided people have wrongly thought they can dissociate us from you. We are not fools. We do know our Shepherds in the faith and we are together at all odds. In unison we will rise up and stand for the truth for it will set us free."* With the amount of support coming through from so many unexpected sources, the weakness and doubt of the previous days dissipated and strength of resolve returned.

As Friday, 13th March drew to a close, John became quite unsettled and agitated. He experienced a very great need to be back with the people in Mzuzu. There were bound to be repercussions for the priests and people because of the letter and they had no bolt-hole to escape the wrath of the police or worse still, that of the Young Pioneers and Youth League. He was the one who had signed the letter. He should be present in Mzuzu if there were a reaction against the people. He phoned the diocesan office, but because they had to assume the phones were tapped, they could not have any sort of meaningful conversation. Except he did learn that rumours abounded that certain priests would be attacked, that certain missions would be attacked. He discussed the situations with Msgr. Castro and other friends who were present. The consensus of opinion was that John should remain under protection in Lilongwe. In the words of one friend: "We do not need martyrs at this time." But the certainty that he ought to return grew ever more insistent and so did his resolve. Eventually it was decided that he should return to Mzuzu the following day. In discussing the travelling arrangements, it was decided that John could not risk flying as the president was due to fly to Blantyre the next morning. John's presence at the airport would be considered inflammatory to say the least. So a decision was taken to travel by road.

The next morning, Saturday, 14th March, dawned bright and clear. John made his goodbyes to Hugh and Danielle Johnson. It was an intensely emotional moment. These people had opened their homes and heart to the Irishman, treating him like a member of their family. For John "their love and graciousness were like pillars on which I could lean." In the discussions the previous night, someone had suggested that John lie in the boot of the car until they were well clear of Lilongwe, a suggestion he immediately dismissed. He did, however, agree to lie on the back seat and be covered with a blanket while Msgr. Castro drove the car.

When they set off, Hugh Johnson accompanied them for about 10km, driving ahead in his own car. Msgr. Castro with John under cover on the back seat, followed directly behind. The city was busy with the pomp and circumstance that usually accompanied Dr. Banda when he was on the move. There were police everywhere. Msgr. Castro maintained a running commentary on everything that was happening around them. When they were well clear of the city, John joined Castro in the front and the rest of the journey was uneventful. They had not travelled the usual route that had the roadblock where he was likely to be killed. They took a longer route around by Lake Malawi. John was seeing the road to Mzuzu with new eyes. He was noting what were possible ambush points and wondering what was around every corner, heaving a sigh of relief when nothing untoward happened.

When they arrived at Katoto, the bishop's house, the reunion with the diocesan secretary, Fr. Chirwa and the bursar, Br. Paul of the Missionaries of Africa (White Fathers) both of whom were showing the strain of the past week, was a joyous and tearful event. There was no vicar general in the diocese – he was still in Ireland with his studies, so the two men had to bear the brunt of any government reaction to the letter. While exchanging their news, Msgr. Castro was called to the telephone. He returned with the news that John had been summoned to Lilongwe the next day to present himself to the Ministry of External Affairs. All four men sat in silence trying to comprehend this twist in events; John could barely assimilate this news. The summons could only mean expulsion. His life since 8th March had become a roller coaster of emotions, but this moment was the deepest trough so far. During the evening, people started calling to the house. Some wanted to pray and show solidarity. But in the solidarity, there was great anger, fear, tears and intense sadness. Just as it was all becoming too much to bear, there was another telephone call to say that it was Msgr. Castro that was required at the office of the Ministry and not John Roche.

Totally exhausted and emotionally wrung out, John decided to retire to bed. Even that was no longer a straightforward act. The immediate advice was not to sleep in his own room. He had to pick a guest-room and in the spartan surroundings with nothing familiar of his own around him, try to find a few hours sleep. Quite against his expectations, John had a restorative night's sleep. As a Malawian proverb says: there is food in sleep.

In the morning he was shown the previous day's edition of the *Malawi News*. In the editorial Archbishop Chiona was described as "*a known illiterate who cannot express himself even when he gives sermons in church.*" It went on "*One wonders what contribution he made, if any, to the research and drafting of the booklet which was obviously the work of sophisticated Mafia-style crooks who carefully chose their words tailored to suit their outfit. Chiona and the other six bishops were simply rubber stamps. That*

117

an Irish Catholic Bishop was the brains behind the drafting of the letter tells the story. It is a calculated international campaign using blind Malawian Bishops to discredit the good name of this country and to instigate Malawians into open rebellion against their leadership. ...We are not prepared to condone any bishop whose aim is to import IRA terrorism into this country to spread the chaotic situations now existing in Northern Ireland by non-conformist and satanic Catholics. ... Any traitor on the payroll of foreign governments to disturb the existing peace and calm in this country must face the clenched fist of the laws of this country without mercy."

This editorial was very disquieting, especially the last sentence. John could feel the might of the government building up its case against him particularly. How it might all end, he could only speculate. With the sense of anger and vulnerability, there was also an odd sense of shame seeing his name in the press in such circumstances.

John decided not to say a public mass on that Sunday morning. He joined one of the communities of sisters in the city for a quiet mass. By lunchtime, it was known in the city that he was back. Messages of solidarity flowed into the house. During the afternoon, the parish clergy came to visit. The priests were buoyed up by the response of the people to the letter. Mass attendance had mushroomed. Non-Catholics were attending mass as a gesture of solidarity and appreciation that the letter had been written and proclaimed. They had no other public forum whereby they could indicate their support. All that was open to them was attendance at mass and the wearing of the rosary. That these people were likely to be watched by the police and Young Pioneers only emphasised their courage.

On 15th March, the Students' Association and the Chaplaincy of the University at Zomba issued a printed leaflet of support 'We support our Bishops', quoting the Malawi penal code on seditious intent and setting out their argument disputing that the pastoral letter could legally be considered seditious. This was in direct defiance of government opinion. The students also marched to church in Zomba in support of the bishops. After prayers that were quite explicit, they then marched back to the University in the company of a group of nurses who had also come to church, in an unprecedented public demonstration. The police fired some shots in the air to disperse the students. A few of them were arrested for a short while and then released. The students continued their protest in support of the bishops and widened the action in support of the idea of multiparty democracy.

John could not sleep at Katoto that night. From then on he had to vary his movements and his sleeping arrangements and be certain that they did not reflect any pattern. Assuming the phones were tapped, Paddy Hagan, the regional superior, who was a fluent speaker of Irish, gave his news updates of what was happening in Lilongwe. While John's skills in spoken Irish had deteriorated over the years, he had no difficulty understanding what he was told. Irish also proved a useful medium for Fr. Pádraig Ó Máille, who used it effectively to get news to his contacts in Ireland, who could then pass it on.

Considering the events of the most turbulent week of his life, John wrote in his diary for 15th March, 1992: "this has been a week I will never forget. I have journeyed from elation to devastation, from pride to shame, from conviction to doubt and finally to some sort of peace. Prayer does not come easy and when it does, the Cross looms large on the screen. I am grateful for the support received, but there is also loneliness – the loneliness of leadership."

Just as the time spent in the EU delegate's house, despite its essential protection, was a type of custody, so also the restriction on John's movements became a wearisome burden. It was an imprisonment of sorts. He had no real freedom of movement. He had to constantly weigh up the potential danger of every action, every journey. He could only travel in convoy. A watchman had to be outside his office and wherever he happened to lay his head at all times. While he acknowledged that the restrictions were part of the price of prophecy, it was a price he had not considered and found it a difficult burden.

Whatever discomforts he was experiencing, there were also the moments of great joy. This was especially when he realised that the people in the villages were paying no attention to what was being said about him on the radio. The broadcasters were well-trained and very skilled at creating exactly the slant they wanted on the reportage. They used their skills well to present the image of John Roche as an IRA terrorist and troublemaker and to create division between him and the bishops, between the bishops and the priests and between the people and their church leaders. The radio reached into every village in the land. Because of transport difficulties and literacy difficulties, the newspapers had a more urban base. The radio, however, was in every community. In some villages there might only be one radio for the whole village, but it was avidly listened to by everyone as they clustered around it. Seeing the government propaganda for exactly what it was, the people christened it the Radio of Lies and listened with greater interest to the BBC World Service, which they dubbed the Radio of Truth. When the Irish travel writer, Dervla Murphy, was passing through Malawi two months later in early May, the country was in the grip of major demonstrations in Lilongwe and Blantyre. In a hotel she found a Malawian trying to tune in the BBC World Service on his transistor, he told her that "we get all our credible information from the BBC."

On 16th March, the Church of Scotland issued a press statement in very strong support of the bishops of Malawi and made it quite clear that Dr. Banda was "*not an Elder of the Church of Scotland in any meaningful sense.*" That a person "*is not properly regarded as an Elder unless they are a member of a kirk session* (local church committee). *Dr. Banda has not been such a member for nearly fifty years.*"

Also on 16th March Amnesty International issued an 'urgent action' request (Afr 36/06/92). It was headed 'Fear of extrajudicial execution,' and listed the seven bishops by name, and was designated for 'general distribution'. The students in the University refused to sit exams scheduled for that day. The police were called in and tear gas was used to disperse the students.

On 20th March, a group of Young Pioneers and Youth League attempted to burn down the Balaka Press which had printed the pastoral letter. The printing press was badly damaged but very little other damaged was caused because the arsonists were interrupted by a group of students who happened to be passing by. In fact two or three of the Young Pioneers were badly beaten up by the students, an action unheard of in Malawi since independence. There were rumours later that the Young Pioneers/Youth League had attempted to lock some workers in the building before setting it on fire.

To counteract the groundswell of opinion in favour of the bishops, the Party organised marches to all cathedral churches in the country. The marches were intended to show support for Dr. Banda and the government, and to denounce the letter and the ever-growing call for multiparty politics. These marches were to be led by the Young Pioneers and the evident hope was that thousands would join in and support them.

The evening before the march was to happen in Mzuzu, John, concerned at what might ensue, met with the commissioner of police in the northern region. The commissioner attacked the letter and all it stood for and told John that he could not guarantee any offer of protection for church property. Knowing well what the Young Pioneers were capable of, John responded by indicating how he saw the role of the police and their duties to the people. Eventually, the commissioner conceded that he would do his best to protect the church property, but advised that John should not be visible. Though he toyed with refusing to do this, he eventually agreed to comply.

The day of the march was very tense. The march would bring the protestors past the bishop's house en route to the cathedral. The house was not immediately visible from the road, and there was some concern Young Pioneers would march on the house. As they approached, their singing could be heard becoming louder and louder. There was an enormous sense of relief when the volume of singing and chanting reduced as the Young Pioneers continued on their way without any detour. They marched to the cathedral of St. Peter and made their protest by singing songs in favour of Kamuzu Banda and against the bishops. They went again without causing any damage. News from the bishops throughout the country indicated that wherever there were protests, they were peaceful and no damage was caused. None of the public joined the marches; in fact, as the Young Pioneers marched to Mzuzu they were ridiculed and jeered. Given the well-justified reputation of the Young Pioneers, this was an extraordinary reaction to them.

On 25th March, there were two significant international affirmations of the bishops and their pastoral letter. The European Union made a declaration criticising the Malawi government's treatment of the bishops and stated, among other comments, that [The European Parliament]: *"welcomes the courageous attitude of the Malawi Catholic Bishops and all those – whether belonging to a church or not – who made their criticisms of current trends in Malawi politics public. Expresses its solidarity with the Malawi people in its search for freedom and development. Appeals to the Malawi Government to exercise tolerance in responding to constructive public criticism and to take steps itself to promote peoples' rights and freedoms ...including appropriate steps to guarantee the safety of the Catholic Bishops and others who spoke out courageously; calls on the Malawi Government to ensure that the bishops are under no from of restriction and are entitled to express their opinion."* This was delivered to Dr. Banda by a high-ranking diplomatic delegation. Also on 25th March the American Ambassador, Mr. Michael Pistor, who had driven to Mzuzu in the official car with all pennants flying, called to the bishop's house at Katoto. He congratulated the bishops on the letter and offered his support and that of his government to John and the other bishops. This very public action of the ambassador would not have gone unnoticed by the authorities.

While the majority of the population supported the letter, not everyone did. This was brought home very vividly to John on a trip back from Nkhata Bay. He had been down by the lake to relax a little and while heading back to Mzuzu he came across a vicious physical fight. He stopped the car, wondering if he should intervene. While deciding what to do, he asked some bystanders what was happening. They told him that the men were fighting over the bishops' letter. Watching the men exchange blows, John realised that while he had received great affirmation from the people, not everyone in Malawi agreed with the letter. It was to be expected that Party workers and those who gained privilege from the Party would be upset by the letter, but to see two ordinary villagers in such conflict was a sobering experience. There were those who felt that Banda's policies, despite their repressive nature, ensured the stability and peace of the country, and they believed that the pastoral letter threatened this stability. While this was the only incident of this nature John witnessed, he heard of other violent reactions throughout the country, though in the context of the widespread acceptance of the letter, they were very limited.

The daily broadcasts of the Malawi Broadcasting Corporation and the print media continued to heap insult upon the bishops. The bishops, taking comfort from the solidarity and support of the people, the students and the priests and religious, remained firm in their conviction that the letter was a necessary and timely document. There was stalemate between the government and the episcopal conference. It became obvious that the situation could not continue.

— Chapter 13 —
Bishops' memo

The pastoral letter had been read out on Sunday 8th March. Three weeks later, by the beginning of April, the government's rage still continued unabated. Malawi's government was receiving very poor publicity in the international media while those Malawians forced into exile and silence were suddenly given a voice. In a response to this, a report in the *Daily Times* of 8th April says "*There is something very sick about the international media, the British Broadcasting Corporation in particular, which of late has decided to "champion the cause" of some few disgruntled failures, who pose as Malawi opposition figures.*" The BBC World Service, more than any other, kept the situation in Malawi on the international stage from the time the letter was read to the people. This public airing of Malawi's problems drove the government into a frenzy of counter-claim and denial. Commenting on reports by the BBC journalist Mike Hall, the *Daily Times* goes on to say "*We are willing to take Mr. Hall's cunning reports as bad verse, and nothing else. As for the dissident claims, we take them as ramblings of opportunists. So too are the "protests" of some governments and organisations who seek to carve some history for themselves out of nothing.*"

Pro-Nuncio Archbishop Leanza called a meeting of the episcopal conference in Blantyre on Wednesday, 1st April. Initially, the occasion was one of high spirits and joy as this was the first time the bishops had met with one another and with the pro-nuncio since their summons to the police headquarters immediately after the letter was read out. Later in the evening they were joined by Archbishop de Andrea from Rome. His presence was a source of puzzlement to the bishops, and while they were very happy to extend hospitality, they were curious as to why he should be present in Malawi. The answer fell like a hammer-blow: both men had come in response to the invitation of the government of Malawi. Desperate to save some dignity in face of the overwhelming support for the letter, the government made overtures, at a very senior level, to the Catholic Church. The shocked bishops asked why they had not been consulted before the two senior churchmen came into the country. Their presence in Malawi would have been noted at once by the police and invited immediate government speculation. After some tense moments, the archbishops delivered their news. They had already met with a delegation of the government, headed by

John Tembo. They had had their meeting with the government before the Malawian bishops even knew they were in the country. The bishops were initially stunned by this revelation. The letter was theirs. They had borne the brunt of the government's disfavour. Their lives had been endangered. That senior churchmen should now open negotiations without any consultation with the episcopal conference was devastating news. In an atmosphere of anger and great disappointment, it was eventually agreed that no further meetings or discussions with the government would take place without the involvement of all the bishops.

Reporting on the meeting that had taken place, the pro-nuncio, Archbishop Leanza, told the conference that the Malawi Congress Party had two demands. One, the letter had to be withdrawn and two, there had to be an apology from the bishops. The immediate reaction of the bishops was that there would be no withdrawal of the letter and there would be no apology. Archbishop De Andrea, the papal envoy, kept repeating that the negotiations with the government were very difficult and they (the archbishops) needed some statement to bring to the next meeting. He requested a memorandum stating the opinions and position of the bishops. Knowing what the Banda government was capable of doing with any such memorandum and explaining this to the archbishops, the bishops said that they could not comply with the request. The pastoral letter had stated all that needed to be said about their opinions and position. They were adamant that there would be no apology from them. The discussions were deadlocked.

The archbishops made it clear that they were not leaving without some kind of statement and after a protracted and heated debate, it was eventually decided that some members of the conference together with the archbishops would draw up a statement which could be further discussed by the bishops. The drafting group was Archbishop Guiseppe Leanza the pro-nuncio, John Roche and a known and trusted lawyer from Blantyre. They sat down together and spent many hours composing a statement. Every word was weighed, every nuance considered. Every sentence needed the question: how would the Party interpret this and how could they twist it to their advantage? Every sentence had to be gauged for its worst possible meaning. Eventually a statement was drawn up and presented to the bishops. Further hours were then spent going through the statement yet again word by word, line by line. Eventually the form of wording was agreed, albeit reluctantly. The bishops were very unhappy that the statement had to be issued at all, but because the papal envoy represented the 'paramount chief', the Malawian bishops would have felt a deep moral obligation to try and accommodate him. John recorded in his diary: "I am not so sure about this memo. The government and Party can use it to suit their agenda."

Given the justified concerns of the bishops, they asked that the archbishops remain in Malawi until the government gave its public reaction, if any, to the statement. The archbishops agreed to this, saying they would stay around for a week or two if that were necessary. The final draft of the memorandum to the government, dated 3rd April 1992, was as follows:

"The Catholic Bishops of Malawi are concerned with the events that have taken place and are still taking place in the country following the issue of the Pastoral Letter, and wish to make the following reflections and observations in order to remove any misinterpretations that have arisen.

1. It is unfortunate that the Bishops' concerns as expressed in the Pastoral Letter have been interpreted in a way that was not intended by the Bishops. The mission of the Church is to proclaim the Gospel and to help in the development of the community of people in all respects.

2. The Church has always worked for peace and harmony among peoples and therefore any ill will, hatred or violence that has followed the publication of the Pastoral Letter is to be regretted. The Pastoral Letter was intended to guide, enlighten and invite the Catholic faithful and indeed all men of goodwill to respond in their lives to the teaching of the Gospel and the social doctrine of the Catholic Church.

3. The Bishops have neither the intention nor the interest to create tensions or confrontations in the country, but to promote peace, justice and development in partnership, and therefore there is no way they could want to be disrespectful to the President.

Precisely as the bishops feared, the government amended the statement somewhat and the final paragraph read as follows: "*The Bishops have neither the intention nor the interest to create tensions or confrontations in the country but to promote peace, justice and development in partnership. Therefore there is no way the Bishops could want to be disrespectful to His Excellency the Life President of the Republic, whom they hold in high esteem.*" The bishops were annoyed with this and felt wholly justified in their opposition to the issue of such a statement.

On Sunday, 5th April, John Roche went to Chitipa in the northern tip of the diocese to celebrate mass with the people. He wanted to visit as many areas as possible to overcome rumours that he had been placed under arrest and, more importantly, to show solidarity with the people. In Chitipa, there was a significant number of 'strangers' in the congregation – these were secret service agents and Party militants. Despite their presence, huge numbers of the faithful gathered to celebrate. There were also many representatives from the other Christian Churches present. After mass, a meal was prepared and a number of women undertook to taste every dish before it was set before John in case it had been poisoned, something not unknown in Malawi. This courageous and selfless act by the very people for whom the pastoral letter was written, was a very humbling experience for John and was to sustain him during the difficult days ahead.

On Wednesday, 8th April, the Malawi Broadcasting Corporation announced that relations with the Catholic bishops had been normalised. The announcement was fair and balanced. When he heard it, John, who was in Rumphi continuing his visitations, was happy enough with it. However, later in the evening Kamuzu Banda spoke on radio and declared that the 'Catholic bishops had come to their senses and had apologised!' The bishops were disgusted with this announcement, knowing full well that the memorandum had given Banda what he needed. A number of them phoned John later that evening expressing their anger and frustration. When the bishops tried to contact Archbishops Leanza and de Andrea, (pro-nuncio and papal envoy, respectively), they discovered that, despite their promises to remain, both men had already left the country. The bishops then decided to request an immediate meeting of the episcopal conference and contacted Archbishop Chiona. The archbishop refused to convene a meeting without giving any particular reason for his refusal. Despite what the bishops had gone through since the proclamation of the letter - the daily government vitriol pouring out of the press and radio, the constant surveillance by government watchers, the constraints on movement, the very real threat of assassination, they remained strong and united. They supported one another, certain of the truth of the pastoral letter. With the sudden and unexpected departure of the senior Church leaders at a critical time, the solidarity showed the first signs of weakening with Archbishop Chiona's refusal to call a meeting of the episcopal conference.

The phone in Katoto started ringing with priests and sisters calling to ask if it was true that the bishops had apologised. The people of the villages and towns, in their innate wisdom, knew that it was the Party's propaganda and dismissed it as such. However, some priests and religious whose critical faculties should have been reasonably finely honed, needed reassurance. When John responded to the umpteenth phone call asking if it were true that the bishops had apologised, his patience snapped and he just asked the person who phoned what they believed themselves.

On 10th April, only two days after the memorandum was made public, the editorial comment in the *Daily Times* was aggressively jubilant in tone as it announced: "*He who laughs last laughs best, so goes an old saying. And today, we laugh in the widest terms at those who wished Malawi and her peace-loving citizens a violent ending to the tension that arose after Malawi Catholic bishops issued a pastoral letter undermining Government.*

These confusionists deserve to be laughed at because soon after the pastoral letter was declared a seditious publication according to the Laws of Malawi, they took it upon themselves to circulate their lies or vandalise property and instil fear and insecurity among the country's law-abiding citizens. In the process, they were joined or further encouraged by foreign hands and irresponsible press. ...It is therefore fortunate that such forces have not gained ground among peace-loving Malawians, thanks to the country's renowned and widely respected policy of Contact and Dialogue. The Holy See, the seat of the Catholic bishops, and the Malawi Government have now normalised their relations, which certainly leaves the dancers of confusions with legs in mid-air. ...the destabilising elements should be brooding in shame at being left behind by the Malawi-Vatican Train of Contact and Dialogue. ... Meanwhile, we continue praising the leadership of this country and the Holy See for putting into practice the contact and dialogue policy. ...In our opinion, the Malawi-Vatican case is a very strong message against destabilisation, and it has the right qualities of true statesmanship and Christianity. It deserves a lot of support." No mention was made of the local bishops, they were completely ignored. It was a very low point for them. An important bulwark of support – that of the universal Church, had been removed and for all the bishops the sense of betrayal was a very deep wound.

Banda's broadcast on 8th April combined with the *Daily Times* editorial of 10th brought reaction from the priests of Zomba diocese who wrote to the bishops expressing their support but suggesting that a further statement from the Church was needed because: "*Otherwise,*

1.   *The people will be misled into thinking that the Bishops have apologised and have withdrawn their letter.*
2.   *Significant people and groups who have risked much in support of the Bishops will be disappointed and disenchanted.*
3.   *The authority of the Bishops will be undermined and they will never again be taken seriously in their leadership position. Besides, their commitment to justice and the social teaching of the church will be doubted.*
4.   *The Church itself will lose respect as a body which leads its people to a better life.*"

Also on 10th April, a letter issued from AMRIM, the association of male religious organisations in Malawi, to the episcopal conference praising the bishops for their leadership and outlining their concern at what they were hearing and reading: *"..we have experienced great happiness and satisfaction at the courage shown by all the bishops. This courage will be an inspiration to us to carry forward the teaching in the letter. We also rejoice that through this pastoral message a greater unity is emerging among Christians. ....However, we view with great concern the confusion caused by the claim that the bishops had apologised. We trust that you will find a way of clarifying your position as a matter of urgency."*

This was to be followed on 14th April by a very similar letter from the priests of Mzuzu diocese. In response, the episcopal conference issued a statement clarifying their position, which was read out at masses on Easter Sunday. 19th April, 1992. This statement gave the text of the memorandum and explained Archbishop de Andrea's role as papal envoy:

"On Monday March 30th 1992, Archbishop Giovanni de Andrea, a special envoy of Pope John Paul II, invited by the Government of Malawi, arrived in Lilongwe. In the following days he held separate discussions with some high-ranking government officials and with the Catholic bishops. After their meeting with the envoy of the Pope, the bishops prepared the following memorandum which they entrusted to Archbishop de Andrea to be presented to H.E. the President." The text of the memorandum followed and the statement concluded: *"Let us repeat once more: the Pastoral Letter is intended to guide, enlighten and invite the Catholic faithful and indeed all men* [sic] *of goodwill to respond in their lives to the teaching of the Gospel and the social doctrine of the Catholic Church."*

— Chapter 14 —

Expulsion

Despite his physical presence in Mzuzu and visits to other towns, rumours still abounded that John had been arrested, had been beaten up or had disappeared. In order to lay these rumours to rest, John decided to continue with his visitations during Holy Week because of its major significance as a time of worship. His first stop, on Palm Sunday, was to Nkhamenya the biggest parish of Mzuzu, in the southern tip of the diocese. This was John's first parish, and as such had a special place in his affections. Though part of Mzuzu diocese, geographically Nkhamenya was in the central region. This was Banda's home territory, and the Malawi Congress Party stronghold. Because of this, the priests of the parish had had a particularly difficult time since the proclamation of the letter, and parishioners had suffered beatings and intimidation. For these reasons, John decided to start the worship of Holy Week in Nkhamenya.

John and the vicar general, Fr. Joseph Zuza, travelled there on Sunday morning. Fr. Zuza had previously been a parish priest in Nkhamenya, so both men were quite well-known there. A huge crowd was waiting for them, so that the ceremonies had to be held outside. The plan was to bless the palms at a local school and then process to the church. Fr. Zuza was master of ceremonies and when introducing the service spoke with deep conviction about Holy Week being a testing time for Church as well as for Jesus, but that the Church, like Christ, would prevail and invited the congregation to be strengthened by truth and courage. The people started ululating and clapping as he spoke. John took up the theme of witness and suffering for that witness in his homily, basing his words around the events of Jesus' death and resurrection. He did not dwell particularly on the pastoral letter as he felt its proclamation had been made. The seeds were sown and would germinate in their own good time.

After mass, they met the church leaders, many of whom had suffered because of the pastoral letter. A leader from one of the mission outstations, a fine strong man, spoke of the 'thrashing' he had received for his support of the bishops and the letter. But more than anything, the word from the people was 'you did the right thing, we support you, please continue.' John records in his diary for that day: "I am always strengthened by the faith and the love of the people – they certainly minister to us in so many ways."

The next major celebration was on Holy Thursday in Mzambazi, a parish in the rural west of the diocese. Again the congregation was large, swelled by members of other Christian churches and the by now familiar sprinkling of secret service agents. After the ceremonies, John and Fr. Zuza met with the church leaders. They, too, had their share of intimidation but it was less than that suffered in Nkhamenya. The people of Mzambazi were also very supportive of the letter and promised to protect the priests and the church against any attack by agents of the government. Again and again the affirmation of the people flowed to the bishops. Banda's broadcast that the bishops had apologised was dismissed by the people for the propaganda that it was. The sense of disappointment and betrayal of the bishops by the senior Church representatives was eased somewhat by the enthusiastic wholehearted support of the people who had borne the brunt of the government disfavour.

On the morning of Good Friday, 17th April, John and Fr. Zuza continued on to Mzimba, the nearest parish to Mzuzu city. He had planned to be in Mzuzu for Easter Saturday and Sunday. Mzimba was the old colonial administrative capital of the northern region. The parish was situated on the fringes of the town itself. As in the other parishes, there was a meeting with the church leadership who had fared a lot better than their compatriots in the central region. Mzimba was ethnically Tumbuka and therefore was quite politicised and the support for the letter was total. The priests of the parish decided to remain in the central mission and partake in the ceremonies. This was unusual, as the priests would normally go to the outstations if the central mission were busy. It was their way of showing solidarity with John and the bishops and identifying publicly with the letter. Br. Joe Eberly of the White Fathers was also present. He had been one of the very few to applaud the letter at the 8.00am English mass in Mzuzu on 8th March. He was involved in development work in the area and was delighted to attend the ceremonies.

The Good Friday ceremonies commenced around 2.00pm. About fifteen minutes into the proceedings there was the sound of a vehicle drawing up outside. John assumed it was some parishioners from the forestry at Chikangawa. There was quite a strong Catholic community there, though small in number they were very committed. If they knew that the bishop was in the area they would make particular efforts to see him. With their rather flexible attitude to time, neither the congregation nor the priests were concerned that proceedings were already under way, and the latecomers were expected to enter and take their places. Nobody came into the church, however, but John saw a seminarian present being called outside. He was not at all concerned by this and continued with the service. About five minutes later, the seminarian returned and beckoned to the parish priest, Fr. Robert Mkandawire, who was at the altar with John. As Fr. Mkandawire left, John was a little concerned, not for himself but for the parish priest. He wondered what had gone so wrong that it was necessary for Fr. Mkandawire to be called away from participating in the ceremony. A few minutes later, Fr. Mkandawire returned, walked up to the sanctuary and told John he was wanted in the parochial house – the police wanted to see him. More puzzled than concerned, John quietly asked Fr. Zuza to continue with the ceremonies, and left the church. Br. Eberly was waiting at the church door and, with a look of concern, wished John well as he headed to the house, alone.

Going into the sitting-room, John came face to face with five men. Two of them were immigration officials and the other three were obviously police. The immigration officials were nervous and uncomfortable. John shook hands with them all and sat down, quite relaxed. He knew one of the immigration men from Mzuzu, who was the first to speak. He nervously explained that they had been told to find John and issue him with a Prohibited Immigrant letter. He did not elaborate. John was stunned. While expulsion was a very real possibility in the early days of the letter, with the announcement that Church-State relations were normalised, John had all but put the possibility from his mind. Acknowledging that he had heard what was said, John said that he had a number of questions, but the official said that they could not answer any questions. When John asked about the normalisation of relations with the Church, nobody said anything. The CID men remained silent throughout the proceedings. There was no sense of personal danger, just a wall of silence. Then the immigration men said they could not answer, they were 'sent men'. When John persisted and asked the source of the order, he was told that it came from the top. When he asked if the 'top' meant the president, the answer was affirmative, and no further comment was made other than to tell him that he had twenty-four hours to leave the country. John then said that as a leader of his people (appealing to the innate sense of respect for the chief by the Malawian) there was no way he could have his affairs sorted within twenty-four hours. But they were intractable. They merely repeated that John had twenty-four hours to leave the country and presented him with the Prohibited Immigrant's letter to sign. John asked what would happen when he arrived at the airport the next day if the flights were fully booked. He was told not to worry that preference was *always* given to a Prohibited Immigrant. John toyed with the idea of not signing the letter, but the tension of the previous six weeks and the sure

131

knowledge that if the government wanted to deport him, they would do so whether he signed or not, all became too much to bear. When he signed the letter, he was given a copy and the immigration official retained a copy. Then for the first time during the whole visit one of the policemen looked at his watch and spoke. He said, "It is now 3.05pm. You are to be out of the country by 3.05pm tomorrow." With that they left.

Taking a few moments to compose himself and hardly able to absorb what had just happened, John made his way back to the church. He said a reassuring word to the worried Br. Eberly and went to the altar. He gave the news of the expulsion *sotto voce* to Fr. Zuza, but did not say anything to the congregation, who must have been puzzled by the movement to and from the altar. They continued with the ceremonies and John preached about the gospel of Good Friday. Afterwards he met the congregation and chatted with them, but still said nothing about his news.

Gathering the priests, sisters and brothers present back to the priest's house, he told them of the expulsion. Seeing their shock, disbelief and the tears of some of the sisters, John began to connect to the physical, emotional and spiritual reality of what was happening to him and realised what it meant to have only twenty-four hours left in the country. It was even less than twenty-four hours, the clock had started ticking at 3.05pm. The stress of the previous six weeks that had been kept at bay while he fulfilled his public leadership role came crashing down on him. The people around him urged him to start making phone calls to see what could be done to halt the expulsion. The first call was to the regional superior, Paddy Hagan, to tell him what had happened. It was difficult to reach him at first because he was involved in church ceremonies. All the while, the minutes were ticking away.

It was no accident that the expulsion order was served on Good Friday afternoon. Offices were closed for the Easter holiday. Even embassies were difficult to contact, having only skeleton staff for the weekend. Paddy Hagan was deeply shocked by the news. He told John that he was also concerned for Pádraig Ó Máille who was recovering from a severe bout of cerebral malaria and was due to fly home to Ireland later that night. As it happened, Ó Máille, much weakened by his illness, was deported as he prepared to board his flight. He was held responsible for orchestrating the student protests against the government in support of the bishops. With all offices closed there was no hope of appeal. There was nothing to do but head back to Mzuzu. They phoned ahead to tell priests what had happened.

The hour-and-half drive back to Mzuzu with Fr. Joseph Zuza was mostly in silence. Normally there would be a lot of conversation between the two men as they got on quite well together, and Fr. Zuza as vicar general was the 'heir apparent' to the diocese of Mzuzu. Now, when more needed to be said than ever before, there was only silence. Eventually they reached the bishop's house at Katoto at around 6.00pm. Fr. Chirwa, the diocesan secretary and Br. Paul, the bursar, were there to meet them. Both men were visibly upset. Word had spread very quickly and very soon other priests and religious based around Mzuzu started calling. There were many tears shed as people tried to come to terms with the shock of the news. By about 11.00pm the visitors began to leave, having arranged to be together with John for a mass the next morning.

John and Fr. Zuza then had to sit down and try to expedite the handover. They hardly knew where to begin. While he was an able replacement, Fr. Zuza was out of touch with the day-to-day running of the diocese because he had been studying in Ireland. Eventually they achieved a transfer of sorts, with Fr. Zuza making quick notes, hoping they would be sufficient. When John phoned the pro-nuncio in Lusaka, Archbishop Leanza had much to offer in platitude but little in empathy.

It was after midnight when John finally got to his room. His secretary, Fr. Chirwa accompanied him to help him pack. As Fr. Chirwa picked clothes and laid them out, John looked around his room and felt to his marrow the truth of the words, 'we have here no lasting city.' He realised that all he wanted to bring with him was the minimum of clothing, his father's rosary beads which had accompanied him throughout his missionary life, some photographs, some prayer books and theology books that had meant something to him. That his life of twenty years in Malawi could be pared down to rosary beads, some photographs and books only accentuated the deep sense of loneliness that assailed him. He got to bed around 3.00am and slept fitfully for a couple of hours. On Saturday morning, he rose at first light and walked around the compound. The loneliness of the previous night had only become more intense. He wondered if he would ever see Malawi again. While he found the appointment of apostolic administrator a very difficult ministry because he never wanted it in the first place, he loved Malawi with a passion. He loved the breathtaking countryside, he loved the spectacular lake, he loved the sounds and the smells of Africa that are like no other, but above all he loved the people of Malawi. Though he was a white European, he felt totally at home in Malawi. He had become rooted in its earth.

At around 9.00am, people started gathering for mass. John was the principal celebrant. In his introduction he spoke of the letter as being a seed planted for the people that needed the care and nurture of the people if it was to grow into a strong tree. About ten minutes into the proceedings, the sisters from St. John's hospital in Mzuzu arrived in with a group of student nurses. As they came in, they began their keening. Their very particular wailing was a sound almost too terrible to endure in its mourning. John reached the lowest point of his misery as the women mourned his passing from them, but he continued with the mass. Afterward, there was very little time for meeting people as he had to get on the road to Lilongwe. He had decided that he was not going to fly out, but go out by road to Zambia. As he prepared to leave, a Malawian he knew quite well, came to John and threw his arms around him and wept on his shoulder. Physical embracing was unusual for men in Malawi and for John there was a strange synchronicity that as one Malawian was expelling him from the country, another Malawian was weeping bitter tears on his shoulder because he had to go.

A number of the religious sisters and brothers had decided to accompany John on his journey. Four cars eventually set off in convoy on the road to Lilongwe.

* * * * *

On the road from Mzuzu to Lilongwe, John travelled with the vicar general, Fr. Joseph Zuza. As on the previous day, they travelled in almost total silence. For Fr. Zuza the journey must have been one of worry and concern at being thrust into full responsibility for the administration of the diocese with barely twenty-four hours notice. For John Roche the journey was one of shock, disbelief, great pain and quiet tears. When the convoy reached the roadblock about half-way along the road from Mzuzu to Lilongwe, where it was believed that John was to be killed shortly after the letter's proclamation, two expatriates stood at the barrier. They came to John's car, which was second in the convoy of four and explained that they were from the British Embassy. They were instructed to accompany him to Zambia. When John told them there was no need for the escort, he was "P.I.'d", was on his way out and that was that, one of the men calmly replied, "John, you know these people, we know these people. We won't be happy until you are in Lusaka." The other interjected dryly, "Until you are in Ireland." With that the enlarged convoy set off again with the security men leading. The truth of the men's words unsettled John. He knew what the government was capable of, knew the truth of the saying "the hand of Kamuzu reaches far," yet to hear it bluntly spelt out was quite a shock to an already deeply traumatised psyche.

At Katete parish, a group of people joined the convoy as it passed through. At Nkhamenya, a large group of the parishioners was waiting on the roadside with the parish priest. Singing and weeping, they implored John to get out of the car so that they could say their farewells. The security men were not happy with this and urged John to return to his car and get moving. He was happy to comply. The encounter was so intensely emotional it was almost beyond his capacity to deal with it. Someone in the crowd called for a blessing; John sketched a motion with his hand, hoping that it would be enough, for his heart was not in it.

When the convoy arrived in Lilongwe, they went immediately to the Catholic Secretariat. Archbishop Chiona and some of the other bishops were present, but were at a loss for words. It was quite obvious that they were deeply shocked at the expulsion. Not all the bishops were there, which was disappointing for John, given their commitment at the beginning of all this, when they said that 'if one went to prison, all would go, if one was expelled they would all be expelled.' Having spent little more than a half-hour at the Secretariat, John made his goodbyes and headed for the regional centre at Chigonekha. None of the bishops offered to accompany him to the border.

At the regional centre, there were some parishioners whom John had known from his time as regional superior. Two of them in particular were deeply upset. They were people John regarded as friends and he appreciated their presence at the centre, especially as it was not in their interests to be publicly associated with a Prohibited Immigrant. The regional superior, Fr. Paddy Hagan, joined what was now the rather large convoy heading to the border at Mchinji and onwards to Chipata in Zambia. John had been moved from his own car to one of the British Embassy cars. It was only an hour and a half's journey to the border, but the security men were more concerned than ever at getting John safely to Zambia.

On the road, once or twice they met cars with the bonnets raised. They may have been totally innocent but the embassy men were taking no chances, and brought their firearms into view leaving them on top of the dashboard. John, disquieted at the sight of the guns, suggested that there was no need for them. As before, when he questioned the security men, he was firmly reminded of the Malawian secret service capabilities. As it happened, they reached the border without incident. When they arrived, the British representative asked for John's passport and said that they would try to treat it as a *corps diplomatique* departure. As it happened, one of the border officials recognised John and asked why he was there, realising that it would be most unusual for a bishop to be out of his diocese during a celebration as important as Easter. John said he needed to meet Bishop

Mazombwe in Chipata, something he would have done several times during his time as apostolic administrator. When the official suggested that it was Holy Saturday and John should be in Mzuzu, John just replied that it was a quick meeting and that he would be back in Mzuzu in time for the Easter celebrations. The official just smiled and stamped the passport with the ordinary exit stamp. The special P.I. stamp was not used. The British Embassy representative retrieved the passport and handed it to John with a twinkle in his eye, and a barely concealed smile. For John, there was a little victory in seeing the passport without the P.I. stamp.

A number of Irish people working in Lilongwe had come to the border with John. He truly appreciated the effort they made to accompany him. He said his goodbyes to them and headed on towards the Zambian border, about six kilometres away, with those who travelled with him. Between Malawi and Zambia in Kachebere, a no-man's land, is St. Anthony's seminary, part of the national seminary. Here the Malawian seminarians study philosophy. The students from Mzuzu diocese gathered with the rector, Fr. Patrick Thwale to bid John farewell. The students, together with the people who had travelled from Mzuzu, those who joined the convoy along the way, formed a group of about fifty people. The farewells were extremely difficult, especially with those who had come all the way from Mzuzu, a journey of six or seven hours. In a state of almost complete exhaustion, John walked into Zambia to the sound of singing and weeping from Malawi.

Bishop Mazombwe was waiting for John and they were joined by the rector of the seminary, Fr. Thwale, whom John had known well. He was taken immediately to the bishop's house, which was about fifteen kilometres away in Chipata. There were some priests there to offer sympathy and concern, but realising John's traumatised emotional state, Bishop Mazombwe, who had made no demands for information, showed John to his room. His gentle presence had been solid and supportive with great tact and understanding.

In his room for barely five minutes, the telephone rang – Reuters were looking for an interview. Almost as soon as the receiver had been replaced, the BBC World Service Programme, *Focus on Faith*, made contact, then the BBC was on looking for an interview. While he was reasonably composed at the time, it was not easy to give the interviews. Only a sense of gratitude for the international publicity that probably saved his life, compelled John to spend the next hour or so giving the interviews. Later he made the call he most wanted, and equally most dreaded, to make. Conscious of the great worry and stress he had unwillingly caused, he phoned his mother in Athlone to tell her that he was safely in Zambia. Her utter bewilderment that the people of Malawi should have treated someone who had loved them and loved their country so much was palpable. Explaining that those responsible were only a minority, albeit a minority with all the power, John knew the sense of his words but they did nothing to lessen their devastation at his fate. They finished up their conversation with the details of John's travel arrangements. Madge Roche told John that she would not go to the airport at Dublin, she did not want to meet him in the glare of the cameras. She would wait for him at home. A woman of great strength and a tireless supporter of his mission, not given to dramatic shows of emotion, Madge Roche had wept during their conversation. Following the phone call, his mother's tearful bewilderment coalesced with his own great loneliness and John experienced the most profound sadness he had ever known.

* * * * *

After the conversation with his mother, John knew that he did not want to spend Easter Sunday morning alone. He had no sense of the Resurrection. He was still rooted in the darkness of Good Friday. Discussing it with Bishop Mazombwe, they arranged to say mass with the Sisters of the Immaculate Conception, who had a house nearby. After a poor night's sleep, constantly thinking about Easter in Mzuzu, he went to the convent to the say mass with the sisters. John spent the morning with them, and had the first glimmerings of resurrection in their quiet presence. They asked no questions, just offered care and support through community. As they went about the ordinary tasks of the day, their community represented continuity and fragile hope for John. In the afternoon, he went to visit some of his own confrères and was glad just to have the compassionate presence of his own brother priests.

On Tuesday 20th April, John flew from Chipata to Lusaka, where the Irish Chargé d'Affaires, Brendan Rogers, and one of John's confrères, Fr. P.J. Breen, were waiting on the tarmac when he arrived. There was no senior Church representative present. There had been a reporter around hoping for an interview, but Mr. Rogers had discouraged him from waiting around by being suitably vague about John's expected time of arrival. When he arrived, John was taken to stay at the Irish Embassy in Lusaka.

The following day, John met with the pro-nuncio, Archbishop Leanza, but it was a rather unproductive meeting. John had hoped for some empathy, some understanding of the enormity of what had happened, but the conversation was soon mired in the verbiage of political and diplomatic merry-go-round and nothing of any substance about the expulsions and their impact was said. Uninspired by the meeting, John drew some comfort from the knowledge that the thrust of the letter would not be lost. Whatever was to happen, Malawi could never be the same again.

John remained in Lusaka for a few days, toying with the idea of going to South Africa for a short holiday before going home. But the imperative to go home to his own place, to his own family, was too strong to resist. Brendan Rogers, who had seen John function quite well on his arrival but begin to deteriorate as the days went on, heard this and he advised him to prepare a press statement. Rogers knew that given his present condition, by the time he arrived in Ireland, John would be in no fit state to meet the press and answer questions; he might say something that he would later regret. John, realising the wisdom of this advice, spent time composing a statement. They then checked it together and agreed upon it. It was a brief statement thanking all those who had supported him and the other bishops, and giving a short resumé of why the expulsion had come about. It concluded: "[The letter] *clearly called for dialogue – dialogue which would ensure the participation of all in the on-going development of the country. It is most regrettable that this call has been misinterpreted. At no point do we, the bishops, take sides in the political debate. That is not our responsibility, nor would we wish it to be so. We offer the wisdom of faith and call for dialogue in trust and openness. It is my hope and prayer that the issues raised in the letter will receive the attention they deserve.*

The events of the last few weeks are still too close and will need further reflection and thought. I ask you to respect my desire to say nothing further at this point. I have left behind in Malawi many dear friends – bishops, priests, sisters and especially the beautiful people of Malawi and I would not like to say anything which would make their situation any more difficult.

May I ask you to continue praying for the church in Malawi and for the leaders of the government."

On arrival at Dublin on the evening of 22nd April, John was met by airport officials and brought through to a private room. Here, he was greeted by the then Archbishop of Dublin, Desmond Connell and Fr. Kieran Birmingham, the Superior General of St. Patrick's Missionary Society. There were also some priests of the Society present, Fr. Derek Byrne who had liased with the Roche family, and Fr. Brendan Cooney, who had taken care of relations with the press. Their welcome was greatly appreciated. With the initial greetings over, John was led to another room into the glare of bright lights and camera flashes. Three of his brothers, Tony, Jim and Peter and his sister, Anne Clune, were there to meet him. The delight in meeting his family was tempered somewhat by the presence of the press, anxious to hear about his experiences. When he finished his statement he declined to answer any questions. This was not received too well by some of those present. John was aware of one journalist slapping the table with annoyance, and wondered if she could even begin to comprehend what he had been through and the fragile emotional condition he was in. His expulsion represented so much more than just a news story. A journalist from the BBC was present, and asked for an interview. John agreed because the BBC more than any other body had kept the plight of Malawi and the bishops to the forefront during the six tumultuous weeks from the publication of the letter to expulsion.

In Malawi, in an article headed 'Abuse of hospitality' the *Daily Times* of 24th April was bullish in its remarks concerning the bishops, and John Roche in particular. Its high-level contact with the Vatican seemed to give the government renewed confidence in its negative comments about the bishops and the letter. *"..Monsignor Roche was here as a guest of the Malawi Government... It was therefore improper of him, and indeed beyond our comprehension of we all [sic] Malawians, that such a man turned around and started behaving in a fashion that was bent on disturbing public order, or, in other words, started biting the same hand that fed him.*

...It should therefore be spelt out in clear terms once more that getting rid of undesirable foreigners is not unique to Malawi. All over the world it is done, as long as the culprits are a thorn to the fabric of public safety and order.

On the question of the remaining Catholic clergymen, whom Monsignor Roche claims are not safe and will be killed, we say this is yet another manifestation of the deportee's fabricative life.

Roche has himself to blame because, apart from being part of the team that authored the pastoral letter – whose subject has now been settled – he continued to undermine the very agreement reached by the Papal Envoy, the Life President and other Malawi Government officials, by engaging in further undesirable activities. We therefore do not see any reason why anyone in his right senses should be pointing a finger of accusation at the deportation, which the monsignor was keen to earn for himself."

There is irony in the fact that the papal envoy's meeting with the delegation headed by John Tembo led to a renewed confidence in the government's power that it expelled John Roche at a time when 'relations were normalised.' At the same time, the meeting contributed to the breakdown of the bishops' solidarity with one another because of the Church's lack of consultation with them. This irony is never more evident then when one reads the words of Cardinal Sodano, Vatican Secretary of

State, in a letter to the bishops dated 19th May, 1992. The letter was an expression of good wishes to the episcopal conference on the ordination of Msgr. Tarcisius Ziyaye as Auxiliary Bishop of Dedza diocese: *"This occasion, full of joy for the church, offers me the welcome opportunity to tell you of the great attention and concern with which the Holy See has followed the development of the events of recent months.*

The visits of Archbishop Guiseppe Leanza, the Papal Representative in Malawi and of Archbishop Giovanni De Andrea - which were meant to show the Holy Father's communion with you, the Bishops of Malawi, in a moment of difficulty and of trial for the life of the Church - were expressions of these sentiments of concern and of a deep sharing in these events."

Leaving the world behind John spent the next two weeks with his family. It was a time of very mixed emotions. Fear for those left behind in Malawi, anger at his expulsion, guilt for what his family had suffered worrying about his safety, relief that he was able to relax, but underlying all a deep emotional weariness. At the end of the fortnight he received word that he had to go to Rome to present a report on all that happened. It was with a certain feeling of relief that he set out for Rome. He could now finally resign his administration of Mzuzu diocese – of what use was an absentee bishop? Whatever was going to happen in Malawi, as a Prohibited Immigrant he was unlikely to see the country again for a long time, if ever. However, Rome had other plans.

The implications of John Roche's expulsion were significant politically and diplomatically for the Vatican. There was an audience with the pope (which was somewhat overshadowed by the presence at the same audience of the rector of a Polish seminary) and John celebrated mass with the pope the following day. These diplomatic expressions of the alignment of the Vatican with the Catholic bishops of Malawi were important, as it could not be seen to accept the expulsion of a senior Church representative for doing nothing other than preaching the tenets of that Church. Therefore, John had to remain as titular head of Mzuzu. He could not see how this kind of administration was possible, but was told that he was to go to Zambia at regular intervals and give instructions and receive reports. For the bureaucrats in Rome, it was a very simple routine task. For John Roche who had to live the reality, it was a very different matter. He had to go to Chipata right up at the border and meet the vicar general of Mzuzu, Fr. Joseph Zuza and leaders of the Church who would come over from Malawi. Every trip to the border was nothing less than the re-opening of a wound. It was inevitable that he would relive the very painful departure of Easter Saturday.

It was also an extremely difficult time for Fr. Zuza who was supposed to be administering the diocese, yet could not take any initiatives because he was not the bishop. Some understanding in the Vatican of the Malawian culture might have helped the situation. No matter how John tried to encourage Fr. Zuza to take the reins, it was not really possible for him to do so, because technically John was still the bishop. He was still the 'chief.' Fr. Zuza's great respect for this fact meant that he could not, in conscience, take John's place. It would have been akin to usurpation. For the people it was just as difficult and confusing. They also would have shown great respect to the bishop. Though Fr. Zuza was in charge, he was not the bishop. Both men existed in a limbo for twenty months and consequently the diocese could not really move forward with plans and programmes.

In between trips to Zambia John tried to keep himself busy. This was difficult because he could not make any plans even to take short renewal courses – he had to be available at short notice to travel to Chipata whenever necessary. The international media and church groups showed quite an interest in him and his situation. He spoke to Israeli and Dutch radio and was invited to England and Scotland to gives talks. The Scottish Presbyterian Church was particularly supportive and very welcoming. Lectures, talks and interviews punctuated the visits to Zambia. And so the uncertainty continued through 1992 and into 1993 without any immediate hope of resolution.

In 1993 there was a conference of the bishops of eastern and central Africa. There was a suggestion from Rome that John should attend. He was reluctant to go because he knew that some of the bishops of Malawi would be there. Because none of them maintained any communication with him since he was expelled, he was not sure how he really felt about meeting them again. He decided, however, that since the trip was suggested by Rome that he had better go since he was still, if in name only, the apostolic administrator of Mzuzu. In Lusaka, he met the four Malawian bishops attending the conference. Meeting them was a tense and difficult occasion. They did not have much to say to one another, despite all they had been through together. One of them told John that they were thinking of him, they might not be the best correspondents, but they were thinking of him. While John accepted the sincerity of the comment, he still had tremendous difficulty with the silence of the bishops at the time of his expulsion. John did not stay with the bishops during the conference, choosing instead to stay in one of the Society's houses with his own confrères.

The conference organisers were interested in getting some individual contributions from the episcopal conferences present, apart from the scheduled papers. They were particularly interested in Sudan, Malawi and Zambia. All three conferences had spoken out in their respective countries. These contributions were not timetabled and were to be taken whenever a suitable opportunity arose. This arose one afternoon when the delegates arrived back after lunch. The chairman called on the Sudan episcopal conference to share their experience. The Archbishop of Khartoum took the podium and spoke for about twenty minutes. A charismatic figure, he held the audience spellbound with his story of gospel witness and what it meant to the people in Sudan. His contribution was very enthusiastically received. The Malawi conference was then called upon. The designated bishop stood up and spoke quietly and sparingly, saying that things were improving. They hoped for the best and asked the prayers of those present, and thus completed his contribution. There was total silence in the room. The contrast of the reaction to that given the previous speaker could not have been greater. Then a voice asked if Monsignor Roche had anything to say and heads turned towards him. Up to this, John had not even considered that he might say anything. He did not have anything prepared, but the meagre response of the Malawi episcopate in the light of all that had gone on caused something to snap in him. All the anger, the hurt, the frustration, the suffering exploded. He berated the Malawi Congress Party, the bishops, the response from the Vatican and anybody else that he felt had not lived up to the witness of the letter. He was totally out of control, an experience new to him, and he did not know how to stop. When he had vented his anger, he paused. Again, there was total silence in the room. The chairman, a Kenyan bishop, gently brought matters to a close acknowledging that things had been very difficult for all concerned. A priest of Mzuzu diocese who was at the conference to give a talk on inculturation, came up to John as he sat down and stayed with him for the rest of the session.

Afterwards there were recriminations from some of those present who received a tongue-lashing, including the pro-nuncio, Arcbishop Leanza. While John was not proud of the manner of his outburst, he believed he said things that he needed to say and told the pro-nuncio as much. Quite apart from getting some things off his chest, the outburst was a clear signal to John that all was not well within him. He thought he was coping with the situation even though he was unhappy with the administration of Mzuzu from a distance. Now he realised that he was not coping at all. His tirade was more a primal scream – his body and spirit telling his intellect that all was not well. However, he could do nothing about it. His problems could not be addressed because he had to head back to Ireland when the conference was over, then prepare for another trip back to Zambia.

In December 1993, John was again in Zambia for a series of meetings with the vicar general and other church leaders. Things were not going well in the diocese and the split leadership was having a very negative effect on the priests and the people and the diocese was already stagnating. When he had finished all the meetings and was preparing to go home to Ireland for Christmas, word came through that his Prohibited Immigrant status had been rescinded. He listened to Radio Malawi that evening and, sure enough, the official word was that Msgr. Roche was free to return to Malawi to resume his pastoral ministry. Even though President Banda still ruled, things had changed considerably in Malawi. Following the impetus of the pastoral letter, political change was afoot. In 1993 there had been a referendum on multiparty politics that had been carried by a two-thirds majority and a general election was planned for 1994. Listening to the radio, John did not know how he felt about the news. He felt neither elation nor sorrow. He felt quite neutral about it all. A vital chain of trust had been badly damaged and he did not know if repair was possible. He did not know if he could re-insert himself into a group that turned its back on him, whether the members of the espiscopal conference did it intentionally or not.

The vicar general, Fr. Joseph Zuza came to Zambia almost immediately to bring John back into Malawi. Even as he crossed the border at Mchinji, John knew that things were not the same; things could never be the same again. Retracing his steps back across the border was a nerve-wracking experience, especially when the immigration officers recognised him and brought him into a separate room. There may have been a multiparty referendum, but Kamuzu Banda was still in charge. The official looked at his passport and was surprised that there was no P.I. stamp. Again, for John there was that little triumph. His passport was returned and he and Fr. Zuza were allowed leave. They set off for Lilongwe, and onwards to Mzuzu. He spent a short time there meeting friends before heading home to Ireland for Christmas as planned.

When John returned, he was quite ambivalent about his relationship with the country. Gone was the joyful exuberance and energy of youth, to be replaced by an older, sadder wisdom. Things had changed in his absence. The priests and parishioners of Mzuzu had made their own journey through major changes in the political landscape without him. John had made his journey through the sense of anger, hurt and betrayal without the people of Mzuzu. They were travelling on rapidly diverging tracks.

A series of meetings and events were organised so that John could re-visit the parishes of the diocese. The female religious and the people of the diocese were very happy to see him. However, the priests were less so. They had organised themselves into an effective lobbying group and were agitating very strongly for an indigenous bishop for Mzuzu. At a meeting held as part of John's re-introduction to Mzuzu, the leader of this group attending with an associate, stood up and made the feelings of their group known. The tenor of the address was neither gentle nor diplomatic and included not only John in its sweep, but all expatriate missionaries. For these men the imperative of the appointment of a local man to the Mzuzu diocese was linked to the sense of white colonisation. The continuing presence of a white missionary as Bishop of Mzuzu was tantamount to a foreign power (the Vatican) saying that the indigenous people did not have the capability to rule themselves. John did not engage the speaker other than to suggest that it was a discussion for another forum.

Throughout 1994 great change was seen in Malawi. Multiparty elections were held and there was a change of government. For John Roche 1994 represented change also. He knew that not only did he want to resign his appointment as apostolic administrator, but that there was no longer a place for him in Malawi. The relationship was irreparably damaged. In discussions with Rome, he had promised to stay until December. Staying long enough to make an orderly hand-over to Fr. Joseph Zuza, John made plans to leave Malawi in December 1994. As always, Rome had different plans, but this time John set his own non-negotiable limits. When he heard nothing about releasing him from his appointment, he telephoned the pro-nuncio to announce that he had completed his task as promised, he had bought his ticket and was heading home. Archbishop Leanza was more than a little chagrined by this news and asked that John wait a few days. When the pro-nuncio made contact again, it was with the request that John stay in Mzuzu until Easter, when the announcement of the new appointment was to be made. Accepting the inevitability of this news, John agreed to stay until then, but added that at Easter he was leaving with or without permission. Just before Holy Week, the announcement was made that Fr. Joseph Zuza, Vicar-General of Mzuzu diocese was to be ordained its bishop on 6th May, 1994.

In the fortnight following Bishops Zuza's ordination, John Roche made his final farewells to Malawi. He visited people and places that had significance for him – the mountains, the plateaux, the incomparable Lake Malawi. As he watched the sunset flame over Lake Malawi on his last evening, John knew with certainty that it would rise again on a new life and on new hope. He knew that within the death of what he had loved, for all its pain, were contained the seeds of resurrection.

Epilogue

The hope that abounded in Malawi following free multi-party elections found expression in the immediate closure of the detention centres and the release of detainees. As the years passed, however, economic conditions in Malawi continued to deteriorate. Lack of accountability by the country's political elite in its use of capital coupled with subsistence farming in exhausted soil and periodic drought has left the population of Malawi very vulnerable. There are unsettling reports that the President, Bakili Muluzi, is seeking to have the constitution changed so that he can run for a third term. As elsewhere in sub-Saharan Africa, HIV/AIDS continues to devastate the population in Malawi. The adult rate of HIV infection is 20% and rising. The average life expectancy has now dropped to 37 years.

As this book goes to press, famine is imminent in Malawi and immediate assistance is essential. Whether or not Malawi receives this aid will depend on the consciences of donor nations who, despite concerns about Malawi's government, cannot avoid their responsibilities towards a long-suffering people who now face the devastation of famine.

—— *Appendix I* ——
Living Our Faith
The Malawi Bishops' lenten pastoral letter

Dear Brothers
and Sisters in Christ,

As we commence this time of the Lord's favour, we, your bishops, greet you in the name of Our Lord and Saviour Jesus Christ.

Introduction

As a community journeying in faith and hope we recognize and accept the Lord's invitation proclaimed again in this time of Lent. On Ash Wednesday we receive ashes with the prayer: *'Repent and believe the Good News.'* This prayer introduces the period of Lent when we shall enter once more into the saving mysteries of the Lord's death and resurrection.

Christ began his public ministry by proclaiming: *'Repent and believe the Gospel' (Mk 1.15).* In this proclamation he states the programme of his ministry; to call all humankind in and through His life, death and resurrection to conversion and witness. People in every age and culture are called to this conversion and to respond in commitment and faith.

In this conviction we, your leaders in the faith, come to share with you what this faith invites us to as a church in the Malawi of to-day. We place this exhortation under the guidance of the Holy Spirit and the patronage of Mary, Queen of Malawi and of Africa.

2

1. The Dignity and Unity of Humankind

Man and woman, created in the image and likeness of God *(Gen 1.26)*, carry in themselves the breath of diivine life. Each created person is in communion with God. He or she is *'sacred'*, enjoying the personal protection of God. Human life is inviolable since it is from God and all human beings are one, springing as they do from a single father, Adam, and a single mother, Eve, *'the mother of all those who live' (Gen 3.20)*.

The unity and dignity of the human race have been definitively sealed in Christ the Son of God who died for all, to unite everyone in one Body. Rejoicing in this truth we proclaim the dignity of every person, the right of each one to freedom and respect. This oneness of the human race also implies equality and the same basic rights for all. These must be solemnly respected and inculcated in every culture, every constitution and every social system.

2. The Church and Society

Because the Church exists in this world it must communicate its understanding of the meaning of human life and of society. As Pope Paul VI says: *'the Church is certainly not willing to restrict her action only to the religious field and disassociate herself from man's temporal problems (The Evangelization of Peoples, no. 34)*.

In this context we joyfully acclaim the progress which has taken place in our country, thanks in great part to the climate of peace and stability which we enjoy. We would, however, fail in our role as religious leaders if we kept silent on areas of concern.

3. The aspiration to greater equality and unity

In our society we are aware of a growing gap between the rich and the poor with regard to expectations, living standards and development. Many people still live in circumstances which are hardly compatible with their dignity as sons and daughters of God. Their life is a struggle for survival. At the same time a minority enjoys the fruits of development and can afford to live in luxury and wealth. We appeal for a more just and equal distribution of the nation's wealth.

Though many basic goods and materials are available, they are beyond the means of many of our people. One of the reasons for this is the deplorable wage structure which exists. For many, the wages they receive are grossly inadequate, e.g. employees in some estates, some domestic workers, brick-makers, etc., and this leads to anger, frustration and hopelessness. Another example of glaring injustice is the price paid to producers, especially subsistence farmers, for some of their crops. We wish to state that every person has a right to a just reward for work done, a wage which will ensure a dignified living for his or her family.

Not only has the worker a right to be paid justly by his employer, but he also has a duty honestly and responsibly to do the work for which he is employed. We would like to remind all Christian workers that their first duty on receiving their earnings is to look to the adequate support of their family. All too often workers spend their salaries for selfish purposes.

Bribery and nepotism are growing in political, economic, and social life. This causes violence and harm to the spirit of our people. Honesty, righteousness, respect, equal opportunity for all: these must be the qualities which guide our nation as it grows and develops into the future.

One of the cornerstones of the nation is "unity". This reflects the will of our Creator that we live in mutual respect and oneness. Tribalism, apartheid (whether economic or social), regionalism and divisions are contrary to the call and truth of humankind. We call all the faithful to celebrate our common birth and destiny in mutual respect, acceptance, justice and love.

4. The right to an adequate education

A society which values its future affords the highest priority to providing education for all its young people. As it is commonly put: *"Young people are the future of the nation"*. A sound education will aim at the following:

i) creating an environment favourable to the physical, emotional, intellectual, relational and spiritual development of pupils.

ii) developing in each student a respect for others and a recognition of civic responsibilities.

iii) promoting the creative potential of students. The unique and diverse talents of every individual are recognized and encouraged.

iv) instilling an appreciation of the students' cultural heritage, i.e. the linguistic, musical and artistic legacy inherited from the past.

v) providing the students with appropriate training and skills which will equip them to make a living in the actual circumstances of our country.

vi) seeking excellence, while aiming to provide education for everyone.

5. Problems of our educational system

At the outset, we wish to record how greatly we esteem and applaud the efforts which have been made by the government to provide education at all levels. The work of the Churches in this field has also contributed greatly to the advancement of our people.

Nevertheless we feel it necessary to draw attention to some of the problems which beset our educational institutions at present:

a. Illiteracy

Illiteracy is one of the principal causes of poverty and lack of development. It cannot be said that we have succeeded in promoting the creative potential of our citizens while there remains a large scale problem of illiteracy in our society. It must be recognized that this is a problem which cannot be solved by state initiatives alone. Since a great responsibility lies with parents, we urge them to recognize their duty by sending their children to school.

b. Falling Standards, Overcrowding and Shortage of Teachers and Materials

It is more and more widely recognized that standards of education are not only not rising, but are actually falling. Clearly there can be little hope of creating an environment favourable to the emotional, intellectual and spiritual development of pupils when schools are grossly overcrowded and suffer from a serious lack of teachers. While the present acute shortage has been made much worse by the policy of requiring all teachers to remain in their own regions, final solutions to these problems will also demand generous increases in the resources made available to education. This will have very practical implications for the way in which our national priorities are established and the budget distributed.

c. Unequal Access to Education

The criteria used in selection of pupils for secondary schools and third-level institutions should be known to all and be seen to operate fairly. Nor should they work to the disadvantage of particular individuals or groups. Access to education should not depend on whom the candidate knows nor on how much money he possesses.

d. Discipline

We believe that indiscipline is a major problem in secondary schools. It will not be solved by threats of punishments. There is a need to examine the underlying reasons for this state of affairs. Among them are:

i. failure of parents to exercise their responsibility towards their children as they grow older.

ii. lack of co-operation between parents and school authorities.

iii. frustration due to poor or uncertain job opportunities.

iv. manipulation of the selection process to include undeserving students.

v. lack of support from higher authorities when action has been taken, or needs to be taken, by the school.

6. Church-State partnership in Education

Improvements will come about in the educational system only if there is mutual trust and genuine partnership between the different interested groups in society, i.e. parents, teachers, the Church and the State. In particular, we recognize the importance of Church-State participation in this area. On the one hand, the Church has a responsibility to support in every way possible the educational goals of the government. On the other, the government has a duty to respect the rights and legitimate aspirations of the Churches. Only through such a mutual recognition of

6

rights and responsibilities will a fruitful partnership between Church and State be realized in practice.

7. Adequate health services for all

Equality among citizens and the demands of justice call for policies which aim to provide adequate health care for all without distinction. The following principles have always guided us in this vital area of concern:

i. Life is sacred. It is a gift from God to be valued from the moment of conception until death.

ii. Human beings can never be reduced to the status of objects. We recognize that our bodies are temples of the Holy Spirit.

iii. Every person is of equal dignity. The value of life is not to be measured by one's age, possessions or position in society.

8. Difficulties experienced in our health services

We wish to pay tribute to the achievements of the government of Malawi in extending health services with the aim of providing the best possible care for all. Particularly worthy of mention has been the establishment of an excellent system of primary health care. The notable contribution of the churches through their extensive network of hospitals and health centres is deserving of special praise.

At the same time we are aware of the severe difficulties which the health services are experiencing at present:

a. Overcrowding and Lack of Personnel

Without doubt the most serious problem is the acute shortage of health centers to cater for the population. One cannot claim to uphold the principle of the sanctity of life if provision has not been made for even minimal health care for every person. This is a priority which a society cannot ignore if it wishes to be a caring and compassionate community. It must be recognized that if this problem is to be tackled, it will demand the allocation of more resources from the State.

b. The Vocation of Caring for the Sick

Caring for the sick is a calling from God of a special dignity and import-ance. It can never be seen as just another job or another way of earning one's living. While we greatly value the generous dedication to service of many of those who work in the medical field, we cannot ignore that the quality of medical care is often seriously inadequate, e.g. patients being unattended to for long periods of time; the lack of commitment on the part of some personnel; the failure to recognize each patient as one's brother or sister in need, etc. We therefore invite all health workers to serve every patient without exception with responsibility and true dedi-cation.

c. Inequality in Medical Treatment

Absolute equality of access to health care for all citizens is difficult to achieve. However, this is an ideal which must always be striven for. The guiding principle determining whether a patient will receive priority treat-ment ought not to be his apparent usefulness or his position in society. Rather, every person, whether rich or poor, educated or not, blood relative or not, has equal right to receive health care. The practice of stealing and re-selling medicines seriously threatens this right.

9. The tragedy of AIDS

It is heartening to note the extensive health education programmes currently in operation in the state. One cannot fail to stress the importance of preventive measures particularly in respect of contagious diseases. The current epidemic of AIDS is a case in point. All recognize that in the present circumstances where no cure for AIDS is available, prevention in the form of health education is the only way of combatting this problem.

We want to encourage the efforts undertaken in that direction and hope they can still be intensified: true facts about the disease should be made public more readily; information made available to all; personnel and resources freed for the treatment and counselling of the victims and their families.
However, preventive methods must respect God's law and enhance the dignity of the human person. It is most regrettable that little attention is paid to the fact that faithfulness to the Gospel's teaching on conjugal

fidelity is the single most effective method of preventing the spread of this tragic illness. We strongly object to the dissemination of the view that the use of condoms is the remedy against this epidemic.

Besides the immorality involved in the indiscriminate distribution and use of condoms, we must be aware how much they contribute to spreading a false sense of security and encouraging a promiscuity which can only aggravate the existing problem. We appeal to Christian parents to protect and counsel their children against such practices and to guide them to a true Christian understanding of sexuality.

10. Participation of all in public life

In their writings to the Christians, both the apostles Peter and Paul note how the Holy Spirit grants the members of the Christian community gifts of all sorts for the benefit of the community. *"On each one of us God's favour has been bestowed in whatever way Christ has allotted it... To some his gift was that they should be apostles; to some prophets; to some evangelists; to some pastors and teachers..."* Whatever the gift, the purpose is one: *"to knit God's holy people together for the work of service to build up the Body of Christ"* (Eph 4,7-16; cf I Pet 4,10-11).

African society has traditionally recognized that what is true of the Church is also true of any society: its strength resides in recognizing the gifts of all and in allowing these gifts to flourish and be used for the building up of the community. *"Mutu umodzi susenza denga".* No one person can claim to have a monopoly of truth and wisdom. No individual - or group of individuals - can pretend to have all the resources needed to guarantee the progress of a nation. *"Mtsinje wopanda miyala susunga madzi".* The contribution of the most humble members is often necessary for the good running of a group. *"Wopusa anaomba ng'oma wochenjera navina".*

11. Freedom of expression and association

Moreover human persons are honoured - and this honour is due to them - whenever they are allowed to search freely for the truth, to voice their opinions and be heard, to engage in creative service of the community in all liberty within the associations of their own choice. Nobody should ever have to suffer reprisals for honestly expressing and living up to their convictions: intellectual, religious or political.

We can only regret that this is not always the case in our country. We can be grateful that freedom of worship is respected; the same freedom does not exist when it comes to translating faith into daily life. Academic freedom is seriously restricted; exposing injustices can be considered a betrayal; revealing some evils of our society is seen as slandering the country; monopoly of mass media and censorship prevent the express-ion of dissenting views; some people have paid dearly for their political opinions; access to public places like markets, hospitals, bus depots, etc., is frequently denied to those who cannot produce a party card; forced donations have become a way of life.

This is most regrettable. It creates an atmosphere of resentment among the citizens. It breeds a climate of mistrust and fear. This fear of harass-ment and mutual suspicion generates a society in which the talents of many lie unused and in which there is little room for initiative.

12. Fostering participation

We urgently call each one of you to respond to this state of affairs and work towards a change of climate. Participation in the life of the country is not only a right; it is also a duty that each Christian should be proud to assume and exercise responsibly. People in positions of authority, in government and administration, have a particular duty to work for the restoration of a climate of trust and openness. However participation will remain a fiction without the existence of adequate channels of expression and action: an independent press, open forums of discussion, free association of citizens for social and political purposes, and the like...

13. "The truth will set you free"

A first step in the restoration of the climate of confidence may be taken by recognizing the true state of the nation. *"The truth will set you free"* (Jn 8,32). These words of Christ do not have an exclusively religious meaning. They also express a deep human reality.

For too long we have refused to see that, besides the praiseworthy achievements of the last decades, our country still suffers from many evils: economic and social progress does not trickle down to the mass of the people; much still remains to be achieved to make adequate education and health services available to all; the AIDS problem presents an incredible challenge; recurrent unfavourable climatic conditions often account for poor crops and subsequent misery for the people....

People will not be scandalized to hear these things; they know them. They will only be grateful that their true needs are recognized and that efforts are made to answer them. Feeding them with slogans and half- truths - or untruths! - only increases their cynicism and their mistrust of government representatives. It gives rise to a culture of rumour mongering. Real progress can only be attained when the true problems and the real needs are identified and all resources are channelled towards solving them.

Let us add here that people in positions of responsiblity have an obligation to know the actual conditions in which their people live and to work tirelessly for their betterment. They should be willing to allow their performance to be judged by the people they serve. Accountability is a quality of any good government. People are entitled to know how their representatives fulfil their duties. No disrespect is shown when citizens ask questions in matters which concern them.

14. A system of justice which works fairly

We would like to draw your attention to another area of life in our society. We cannot ignore or turn a blind eye to our people's experience of unfairness and injustice, for example those who, losing their land without fair compensation, are deprived of their livelihood, or those of our brothers and sisters who are imprisoned without knowing when their cases will be heard.

In a just society, a citizen must have easy access to an independent and impartial court of justice whenever his rights are threatened or violated. In particular, before a penalty is imposed, it is in the interest of justice and human dignity that the accused be informed in good time of the charge against him and be granted opportunity for a fair trial, and where necessary, the possibility of legal counsel. We call upon all and particularly those responsible for the administration of justice to ensure not only that procedures are respected but also that impartial judgment is rendered to the accused person. This will only be possible if the administration of justice is independent of external influence, political or other. Our bond of brotherhood and sisterhood in the one body of Christ and our solidarity as a people should, in love, compel us to hunger for the justice and righteousness of the Lord in our society.

In this context, we recall the words of Jesus at the beginning of his ministry:
"The Spirit of the Lord is on me, for he has anointed me to bring the good news to the afflicted. He has sent me to proclaim liberty to captives, sight to the blind, to let the oppressed go free, and to proclaim a year of favour from the Lord" (Luke 4,18-19).

This appeal for fair treatment should also be heard within the Church. We want to recall the importance of adhering to procedures which have been instituted to promote justice and protect the rights of the faithful. Our Church communities do need well established and competent forums for hearing various cases, complaints and grievances of their members. Those of us who have to pronounce judgment on persons and situations are to view the exercise of their authority as a service of the truth for the common good as well as for the well-being of the individual. In particular, we exhort the people of God to respect the right of defence of those accused of having committed offences.

Conclusion

15. **"Love tenderly, act justly, walk humbly with your God"** *(Micah 6,8)*

The issues raised in this letter will obviously require an ongoing and more in depth reflection. It is the Church's mission to preach the Gospel which effects the redemption of the human race and its liberation from every oppressive situation, be it hunger, ignorance, blindness, despair, paralyzing fear, etc. Like Jesus, the advocate of the poor and the oppressed, the believing community is invited, at times obliged in justice, to show in action a preferential love for the economically disadvantaged, the voice-less who live in situations of hopelessness.

The human rights and duties identified in this pastoral letter for our reflection are only some of the issues that our God invites us to consider seriously. In our response to God, we humbly recognize that though a gifted and blessed people, we are not a perfect community. If some of our personal weaknesses, biases and ambitions are not purified by the word of God and just laws, they can very easily destroy peace and harmony in our societies and communities. We hope that our message will deepen in all of us the experience of conversion and the desire for the truth and the light of Christ. This will prepare us for the worthy celebration of Easter, the feast of the risen Lord in whom we see ourselves as a risen people with dignity restored.

Archbishop	J. Chiona
Bishop	F. Mkhori
Bishop	M.A. Chimole
Bishop	A. Assolari
Bishop	A. Chamgwera
Bishop	G. M. Chisendera
Monsignor	J. Roche

BIBLIOGRAPHY

Davidson, Basil. The Black man's burden: Africa and the curse of the nation-state. London: James Curry, 1992.

Duignan Peter and Robert H. Jackson, eds. Politcs & Government in African States 1960-1985. London: Croom Helm, 1986.

Hobsbawm, E.J. The Age of revolution 1789-1848. London: Cardinal (an imprint of Sphere Books Ltd.), 1988.

Hobsbawm, E.J. The Age of capital 1848-1875. London: Cardinal (an imprint of Sphere Books Ltd.), 1988.

Lwanda, John. Promises, power, politics and poverty: democratic transition in Malawi (1961-1999). Glasgow: Dudu Nsomba Publications, 1997.

Lwanda, John. Kamuzu Banda of Malawi: a study in promise, power and analsyis, Malawi under Dr. Banda (1961-1993). Glasgow: Dudu Nsomba Publications, 1993.

McGrady, Andrew G. "Cultural Ecology and Media Ethics: a perspective from a Christian philosophy of communication." In Eoin G. Cassidy and Andrew G. McGrady, eds. Media and the Marketplace: ethical perspectives. Dublin: Institute of Public Administration, 2001.

Manda, Mtafu Almiton Zeleza. The state and the labour in Malwai. Glasgow: Dudu Nsomba Publications, 2000.

Merriman, John. A History of Modern Europe, Volume 2: From the French revolution to the present. New York: W.W. Norton & Company, 1996.

Mkamanga, Emily. Suffering in silence: Malawi women's 30 year dance with Dr. Banda. Glasgow: Dudu Nsomba Publications, 2000.

Mkandawire, Dr. Austin. Living my destiny: a medical and historical narrative. Glasgow: Dudu Nsomba Publications, 1998.

Murphy, Dervla. The Ukimwi Road: from Kenya to Zambia. London: Flamingo, 1993.

Nasimiyu-Wasike, Anne, LSOSF. "Africa and the North: Dialogue of Solidarity." In Walter von Holzen and Seán Fagan, eds. Africa the Kairos of a Synod: symposium on Africa. Rome: SEDOS, 1994.

Nyerere, Julius K. Man and Development. Dar es Salaam: Oxford University Press, 1974.

Oliver, Roland and G.N. Sanderson, eds. The Cambridge History of Africa: Vol.6 1870 to 1905. Cambridge: Cambridge University Press, 1985.

Ó Máille, Pádraig. Living dangerously: a memoir of political change in Malawi. Glasgow: Dudu Nsomba Publications, 1999.

Pakenham, Thomas. The Scramble for Africa 1876-1912. London: Abacus, 1991.

Rafael, B.R. A Short History of Malawi. Limbe: Popular Publications, 1988.

Ransford, Oliver. Livingstone's Lake: the drama of Nyasa. London: John Murray, 1966.

Short, Philip. Banda. London: Routledge, Kegan Paul, 1974.

Thomson, David. Europe since Napoleon. Middlesex: Penguin Books, 1966.

Turnbull, Colin. The Lonely African. New York: Touchstone (an imprint of Simon & Schuster), 1987.

White, Sheldon and Barbara Notkin White. Childhood: pathways of discovery. London: Harper & Row, 1980.

Williams, T. David. Malawi: the politics of despair. Ithaca and London: Cornell University Press, 1978.

www.greatepicbooks.com/epics/July1996.html

www.geocities.com/athens/parthenon/8409/malawi.html

INDEX